HOW TO PUT **TEN** HOURS IN AN EIGHT HOUR DAY

by Kay Johnson
edited by Susan Harrison

Published by EduTrain Press, 5011 NW 96th Drive, Coral Springs, Florida 33067. First edition.
Second printing.

ISBN: 0-9638445-0-4

ACKNOWLEDGMENTS

In life we rarely, if ever, do things of significance by ourselves. Generally, we are entwined with others to accomplish life's greatest moments. So I dedicate this book to my family — Phil, Phillip, and Ruthie! They have taught me to live fully with purpose!

TABLE OF CONTENTS

Introduction:
Looking In The
Rear View Mirror

Some experts predicted that industrial automation would bring greater leisure hours to American workers, but the reverse is true. Just two decades ago, forty-hour work weeks were the norm. Today, most executives routinely work 50 to 60 hours a week.

In my work as a management consultant, I meet thousands of people every year who are suffering from a time crunch — no time for vacations, for family, for planning or for fun. Work is sapping not only their time, but their energy. Their lives are out of balance, but they don't know what to do about it.

Many executives face a daily time crunch
that leaves them exhausted and unfulfilled.

This book is about regaining control of your time. It is filled with practical pointers, gleaned from years of research and consulting, that will help busy executives add minutes and hours to each day. But what good is adding time to your schedule if it's not channeled into something meaningful or productive? That's why I begin with the one key principle to successful time management: looking in the rear view mirror.

THE REAR VIEW MIRROR

A number of years ago, I was involved in a terrible automobile accident. Recuperation from this accident took three months in a bed, lying flat on my back. After only three days of watching *Oprah* and *Donahue* and reading Sidney Sheldon novels, I was bored to tears. Then my father introduced me to the idea of looking at life through a rear view mirror.

During a visit, he said, "You know, Kay, this will probably be the only time in your life when you will have 87 days with no responsibilities for anybody but yourself. You will not be at anyone's command but your own. You can either lie in bed and be miserable or use this time productively."

I asked how I could possibly be productive, lying flat on my back in bed.

"You could plan your life," he said. "Most of us take a very short-term view, and I think you need to look at life through your rear view mirror."

"My *what?*"

"Your rear view mirror," he answered.

His rear view mirror perspective proved to be one of the most powerful concepts I've ever learned. My father challenged me to imagine myself at my grandmother's age of 102 and to look backward at my imaginary lifetime.

"Suppose someone from the newspaper comes to interview you," he said. "What would you like to say made your life successful? Look at the big picture. What would you really like to do with your life?"

The rear view mirror helps you see what's important.

That concept — looking at life through a rear view mirror — hit me hard. I call it a BGO, a Blinding Glimpse of the Obvious. My father was very good at giving his children BGOs. This idea made a lot of sense to me. Figure out what you want to accomplish in life, then determine how to do it.

When you define your life goals, it becomes easier to weed out those activities that are bogging you down. Decisions become easier when you are focused on the finish line.

I decided that day to give it a try. My father said he'd be back in two or three weeks to see what I had learned. I realized setting life goals is much more difficult than it seems. By the time he returned, though, I had decided on three things: I wanted to run my own business, to learn to fly a plane and to build my relationships as a wife, mother and friend. Now, years later, I can say I've accomplished the first two. And I'm still working on the third, as well as a new set of goals.

When you know where you're going, it's easier to get there.

Why talk about rear view mirrors in a book on time management? The rear view mirror gives you a sense for what is important. In trying to look backward at 100 years on earth, you rise above the storm clouds of daily life. You can more easily decide what is truly important away from the pull of your current activities. Once you see what you'd like to accomplish in a lifetime, you can determine the best use of your time week by week and day by day. By the same token, you can better identify time wasters. The rear view mirror keeps you from endlessly spinning your wheels. Let's take a quick look at time.

THE BANK ACCOUNT OF LIFE

Time is our ultimate resource. I used to think the most valuable asset was money, but that isn't the case. We can always earn more dollars for the financial bank account. You can borrow, mortgage, take an extra job, or cut expenses to change your bottom line. The "bank account" of life, however, is finite. You cannot borrow, rent, buy or even steal more time.

A few calculations can tell you how much time you have left in your bank account of life. The average life expectancy for an American female is 79 years, for males, 72 years.

Subtracting your age from your life expectancy gives you the number of plannable years you have left. For instance a man of 40 could expect to live approximately 32 more years. Multiplying 365, the number of days in a year, by your number of plannable years yields the number of days you have left to accomplish your goals. Our man of 40 will have 11,680 days left if he lives an average length of time.

Here's a formula for you:

Average Life Expectancy	Current Age	Plannable Years	Days In A Year	Plannable Days
Male: **72** − ___	=	___	x **365** =	___
Female: **79** − ___	=	___	x **365** =	___

The point of this calculation is to show you the value of time. I like to break the formula down even further to hours. It's easy to "lose" an hour here and an hour there. But you've only got a finite number of hours in your account. It wasn't until I did this calculation that I understood time really is the ultimate resource. I may actually have more hours than calculated or fewer, but changing the amount is for the most part out of my hands. There are things I can do to affect this amount on a long-term basis — diet, nutrition, and exercise, for example — but what is more controllable today is how I use the time I have.

The way you use this bank account of life is the difference between successful and unsuccessful people. How we spend each hour, day, and week makes all the difference. Because you never know whether you've got one day or 11,000 days in your account, you have to make each day have impact. Using your rear view mirror will help you focus on your true priorities.

My grandmother could tell fabulous stories about going to church as a young girl in a horse-drawn buggy, yet she lived to see us put a man on the moon. She used to tell me, "Life is not a dress rehearsal. This is the only chance you get, and I've really enjoyed my life."

Like my grandmother, I want to be able to look back with no regrets and to say I've really enjoyed my life. Improving our time management gives us more time to do those things we really want to do. And checking in the rear view mirror periodically will help us stay on track.

LOOKING FORWARD

The 200 pointers in the following chapters will show you how to add time to your day. How you invest that "extra" time is up to you.

Other than encouraging you to set goals, this book won't try to change your human nature. You'll find no time logs or worksheets or self-evaluation tests to complete. We'll look at the major areas of an executive's life including paperwork, travel, meetings and people from a practical, how-to perspective.

These tips are to help you use the time you've got — your resource — the best way possible. I hope these ideas will bring you more success in the years to come and help you to be productive on and off the job.

JUST DO IT

Managing your time successfully will require a good measure of self-discipline and a willingness to change. Many executives are eager to improve their management of time, but they resist change — a normal response. Clinging to their traditional systems, the ones that got them where they are today, they stay in their comfort zones. But with executives averaging 50- to 60-hour work weeks and competition for top spots intensifying, they must take steps to become more productive in fewer hours.

Many business people labor under the illusion that working harder and longer will make them more successful. And it is an illusion! Increasing the length of your business days and working longer hours only leads to burn out, boredom with

The goal of time management is to reduce the hours you work, while improving your output.

the job, and poor decision making. Conversely, the goal of time management is to reduce or maintain your hours, while improving the quality of your work.

Of course you *can* just log an increasing number of hours at the office. A recent client of mine refused to take even one day off during the Christmas holidays. He said he felt too anxious being away from work that long. Another client, a physician, told me he often sleeps at his workplace. Because of a full schedule at the hospital, he feels compelled to work harder at the office. His co-workers consider him disorganized and emotional, and they have little respect for his leadership style. The real kicker is that the doctor wants to lead by example! But no one is following, because the example isn't a positive one.

If, like these executives, you want to spend all your time at the office, you don't need this book. My assumption is that most of you want to have a life away from work. Managing your time well and working more effectively should give you the opportunity and the freedom of conscience to enjoy some leisure time.

Rather than just dreaming of family dinners and cycling the back roads, muster the courage to change. And then just do it. You'll be glad you did.

Old habits die hard.
Allow 21-28 days to make a change routine.

Remember that these techniques will frequently challenge the familiar processes of your work. Old habits will need to be replaced with new ones. And they die hard. Most habits stem from repetition and reinforcement. Once you have decided to change a habit, it takes about 21 days of repetition before the change becomes routine. When trying to incorporate the pointers suggested in these pages, commit yourself to practice for 21 days. If the habit you are breaking is a longstanding one, give yourself even longer to make it a part of your daily life. The rewards will be far greater than the effort required.

Give yourself positive reminders. Place notes on your bathroom mirror, the dashboard of your car, or your calendar to constantly reinforce the change. On my telephone receiver I have a note that says, "Thin and Win" to remind me to eat less fat in my diet. Each time I pick up the receiver, I am reminded of the habit I need to change.

Use positive phrases in these notes. For instance, my note says "Thin and Win," not "Don't Eat Sweets." The tip is phrased positively, which helps in changing a long-standing habit. Think of your work habits, what is working and what's not. Then post notes for yourself to increase your success.

Not only are executives generally short on time for book reading, but it would be too overwhelming to try to incorporate all these ideas at once. Adopt these pointers one step at a time. Allow some time between chapters, or even between pointers, to adjust before moving on.

The first step you'll want to take is learning how to plan your days and weeks. This chapter introduces the best time-saving device — the calendar — and the backbone of time management — scheduling.

USE A CALENDAR

Just like a certain charge card advertises, don't leave home without it. A detailed calendar will save you time and frustration when used on a daily basis.

At the beginning of each year, pencil in commitments that are already scheduled such as conferences, vacations or board meetings. At the beginning of each month, jot down all recurring activities such as staff meetings or sales reviews. During busy times it's easy to forget these tasks if they are not written. On a daily basis, record all appointments, activities, and goals. Be sure to reserve some time for reading, writing and paperwork.

I like a wallet-sized calendar that gives me a full page for every day. A vertical half of each page is devoted to scheduling by the hour or minute. The other half is for making notes and recording details. Calendars come in a variety of sizes and formats. Find the one best suited to your needs.

MAKE IT YOUR CONSTANT COMPANION

Keep your calendar with you, and you'll know at a glance when you're available and when you're not. You can avoid accidentally scheduling two commitments for the same time and having to take time to reschedule one of them. And when someone invites you out or requests a meeting, you don't have to say, "Let me check, and I'll call you back." Just pull out your calendar and respond on the spot. Confirmation and follow-up becomes the other person's responsibility, rather than the monkey on your back.

The calendar even helps out in my free time. For instance, if I'm in line at the gas station and suddenly remember my mother's birthday is next Wednesday, I can make a note in the calendar to call her that day.

CHOOSE A FRIENDLY SYSTEM

Select a calendar system that is user-friendly — easy to carry and available for quick reference. Many computerized systems offer few, if any, advantages over traditional handwritten varieties. Unless you have a laptop computer, your calendar can't travel with you. And unless your computer runs all day, it takes time to pull the program up on the monitor.

Whatever system you adopt, be sure your secretary can access it for scheduling appointments. If you choose a computer system, train your secretary to use it. If using the traditional calendar, make sure it's easily seen on your desk and not tucked in a drawer.

KEEP A DAILY "TO DO" LIST

Plan a reasonable list of things that you want to accomplish each day. Every evening before going home, I check my calendar and tickler file and make a TO DO list for the next day. This list can easily be kept with your calendar or in your calendar for quick reference. Include everything for the day such as meetings, appointments and projects.

A TO DO list keeps your focus on priorities.

A TO DO list keeps you focused on where you are supposed to be and what your priorities are. By forcing you to think in an orderly fashion, the list stops you from jumping randomly from one project to another or simply doing whatever task lies at the top of your in-basket.

MAKE AN APPOINTMENT WITH YOURSELF

Allowing time every day for planning walks hand in hand with making TO DO lists. You need to schedule time regularly to *think*. It's easy to try doing everything right, but harder to do the right things. Without time for reflection, you may find yourself whittling away at a pile of demanding, inconsequential tasks and largely ignoring critical issues. Block out time — even just five minutes — on your calendar every other day to evaluate your activities in light of your priorities and goals.

PLAN TWO RETREATS

Take two days out of every year to get away from the office by yourself for long-range planning. From a professional perspective, look in your rear view mirror and determine what your priorities are. Identify goals for the next six months, two years, and five years. You may even want to look farther ahead.

Management consultant Phyllis Thompson notes that quality expert W. Edwards Deming measures the potential level of promotability for an executive by how far out he or she can think and do long-range planning. Deming is the industrial management expert often credited with turning around Japanese business in the 1950s and laying the groundwork for that country's manufacturing success today. When Japanese executives discuss long-range planning, they usually look 25 to 50 years down the road.

Setting goals is critical to your success.

Write down your goals and refer to them regularly. Post them somewhere you can see them every day. Staying on track this way will save you hours of lost time traveling the side roads.

Be sure that the priorities you identify are in sync with those of your employer. In my research, I frequently see overlapping jobs, fuzzy job descriptions, and managers and employers with differing perspectives. This confusion creates time problems and conflict. If necessary, meet with your boss and ask, "How do you spell SUCCESS?" Identify priorities together. A clear understanding of your job channels your energies in the right direction.

RATE YOUR "TO DO" LIST

As you write your daily TO DO list, assign each item a rating of **A**, **B**, or **C**. The **A** rating marks top priority items, those tasks that must be done before the day is over. **B** denotes routine activities, ordinarily done during the course of business. **C** is for tasks you would like to do, but are not essential.

A = Critical   B = Routine   C = Optional

Once **ABC**s are assigned, order the items. The first activity of your day should be **A-1**, the second **A-2**, and continue through the last **C** item. The next day, as you complete an item on the list, draw a vertical line to the left of it. By the end of the day, you should have a straight line down your calendar. You can tell immediately what progress has been made. **A** items must be completed before leaving the office. **B**s can be carried forward. If you routinely move **B**s, it's a signal that you are either procrastinating or overscheduling your day.

STUDY YOUR "TO DO" LIST

Studying the list will help you understand what your patterns are. Are there certain tasks that never seem to get done? This **ABC** system showed that I tend to procrastinate on larger projects. If you never reach the end of your list, you may be scheduling too much in each day. Once you identify a weakness, you can figure out a way to correct it.

SCHEDULE NO MORE THAN 50% OF YOUR DAY

My first TO DO lists were way too extensive. I was frustrated and worn out by the end of a day. Naively scheduling myself from daybreak to bedtime, I allowed no time to talk to people, no time for interruptions, and no time for mistakes. As a result, I rushed frantically from place to place, always in too big a hurry to listen to anyone.

Schedule no more than 50 percent of your day so you can cope with the unexpected. TO DO lists should be manageable and realistic. When you are harried and rushed, you tend to make mistakes and make poor decisions.

GROUP RELATED ACTIVITIES

Many people waste time jumping from one activity to another. They make a call, write a letter, file papers, make another call and jump activities throughout the day. Grouping similar activities will keep you moving with less transitional time wasted.

Reserve blocks of time on your calendar for office work and keep them, except for critical events. Within that office time, do related activities together. For instance, return all your phone calls in succession, before moving on to correspondence or mail or another task.

Also try to schedule meetings on one or two mornings a week, rather than randomly throughout the day or week. I prefer Tuesdays for meetings. Whenever I have a choice I will suggest Tuesdays, rather than saying, "What looks good to you?"

RECORD THE SPECIFICS

Use only one calendar and make entries specific. An appointment should include not only the time, but also a name, address, directions, if needed, a phone number, and the goal or purpose of the meeting.

DO ONE THING IMPERFECTLY EVERY DAY

According to experts, one of the most common reasons people fail is trying to do everything perfectly. Some people believe they must give 100 percent effort all the time. But you must distinguish between tasks that can be 80 percent and those that must be 100 percent.

Examine your TO DO list and determine what can be done at less than 100 percent. Give your best to what's important and don't waste time dotting is and crossing ts for inconsequential items.

DIVIDE BIG PROJECTS INTO MUNCHIES

Many of my clients put off big projects, hoping in vain for a large chunk of time to start them. Such chunks just won't happen, unless they work on the weekends or on free time. Break big projects into *munchies*, small tasks that can be done in short time periods. If you have a one-hour project to complete, divide it into four 15-minute segments. Then schedule these segments in your calendar.

Suppose a report will take about an hour to prepare. In your calendar, you might schedule four segments for the week as follows:

Monday
11:45 - 12:00   Outline Report

Tuesday
8:30 - 8:45   Collect Data

Wednesday
5:00 - 5:15   Draft Report

Friday
8:30 - 8:45   Edit/Complete Report

TAKE LATE LUNCHES

Restaurants are busiest between 11:30 a.m. and 1 p.m. If company policy allows, plan your lunch hour to begin at 1:15 or 1:30 in the afternoon. By then, crowds are dissipating. You'll get better service, a quieter atmosphere, and avoid lines at the same time.

SCHEDULE TIMELY APPOINTMENTS

Scheduling appointments at certain times of the day can alleviate spending too much time in waiting rooms or lobbies. Executives are more likely to see you promptly early in the day, before late meetings or office crises throw them off schedule. Medical offices usually run closest to schedule early in the morning and just after lunch. These early afternoon appointments are best for my schedule since they coincide with my later lunch hour. Retail businesses frequently hit lulls in activity in mid-morning and mid-afternoon. During these hours you'll face fewer lines and less waiting than at other times of the day.

AVOID RUSH HOUR

If you drive to and from work, avoid rush hours by arriving early or working late. Schedule any out-of-office appointments that are nearer your home than your office for first thing in the morning and go straight from home to your appointment. In the evenings, schedule those appointments at the end of the day and head home afterwards. You can always contact the office by phone, if needed.

Using Your Head To Stay Ahead

My research shows that successful people are far from haphazard on the job. Most of them are very well organized with systematic methods for accomplishing their work. For some people, organization comes naturally. For others, like me, it's an effort.

Effective organization involves not only your physical surroundings and activities, but your thought processes as well. Much of this book outlines simple, what I call *active*, methods for saving time. These *active* pointers involve changes that are easy to make and bear nearly instantaneous results.

Most people choose the active pointers, the small things you can do to make a quick difference. But there is another part of the process, the *reflective* aspects, that are just as important and often even more important.

According to a *Wall Street Journal* article, there are five major reasons for failure among executives. Every reason involves an ongoing way of thinking:

1 *Inability to get along, especially with subordinates.* Poor interpersonal skills constitute the biggest reason for failure.

2 *The "me only" syndrome.* Managers become too preoccupied with themselves — how much recognition they are getting,

how much they are earning, and how rapidly they are promoted.

3 *Failure to adapt.* Many executives cling to a once-successful style or strategy even after the strategy stops producing results.

4 *Fear of action.* Although diligent workers, executives are sometimes indecisive, avoiding action in order to prevent failure.

5 *Inability to rebound.* A number of executives, especially those who were successful early in their careers, react to failure by being defensive or trying to hide their mistakes. Instead of accepting criticism as a challenge, they reply with excuses or a cover-up. Others drag out disappointments or setbacks. They go over and over them, often for years, when they should learn from the experience and move on.

Overcoming these ingrained patterns with positive thinking, creative planning and the other methods suggested in this chapter will help you not only avoid failure, but also bounce back when you do suffer a setback. Dragging things out takes time, valuable effort, and is unproductive. For high energy extroverts, adopting these reflective activities will be especially challenging as they involve less tangible results and take longer to implement than other techniques. Their impact, however, is as important and far-reaching as the active steps.

THINK CREATIVELY
Give yourself at least three approaches for every problem or assignment to avoid "digging yourself in" with only one approach. Learn to take off mental blinders, brainstorm, and create more alternatives, look at options to avoid too many trips back to the drawing board.

For example, a city Board of Realtors hired my firm to educate its members in leadership skills. We could have met with them and given them a recommended format for the conference. Instead we brought several possibilities to the table: a keynote address to everyone in leadership, a series of meetings with board members, and a seminar with the board and top committee members. We discussed all three approaches and determined which was the best format for that organization. If we had arrived at our meeting with only one possibility, chances are good that the idea would have been rejected for one reason or another. Then we would have had to rethink and regroup at a later date to solve the problem.

PRACTICE PROBLEM SOLVING

Plan one hour a week to hone your problem-solving skills and to take off "mental blinders." It's a fun way to increase your productivity. You can find appropriate puzzles and games in books available at your local bookstore. Select a few to work on now and then to keep your mind sharp. And you can involve your staff as well. Use the puzzles as ice breakers at meetings to get everyone thinking creatively from the very beginning.

Sharpen your thinking with problem-solving activities.

A vice president at Sara Lee Corporation requested we start a meeting with an energizing look at problem solving. We divided the 18 participants into three teams and gave them four short puzzles to solve. When a group had the answer, they had to shout out, "We've got it!" as they did "the Wave."

They had a great time while learning to look for creative solutions. The following two days were devoted to analyzing business opportunities and developing possible solutions. Participating executives left the conference fired up about new concepts, new approaches, and new strategies. They were motivated, had built communication bridges with each other and were ready to tackle new activities. Now that department starts many of their meetings with a problem-solving activity.

This approach doesn't take long, just three to five minutes. And it can help your group learn that planning different approaches and alternatives will save time and money.

PREPARE FOR THE WORST — AND THE BEST

When teaching negotiating at Harvard Law School, Professor Roger Fisher recommends determining your BATNA, Best Alternative to a Negotiated Agreement, and your WATNA, Worst Alternative to a Negotiated Agreement. The BATNA is your greatest hope for an outcome, the WATNA the deal breaker or point at which you will walk away. In terms of time management, plan for the best and worst scenarios at a meeting or conference. Think of the best case and how you can accomplish your goal. Then plan the worst case, how you can prevent it and defend against it.

The Japanese are great at planning their WATNA, and they usually have contingency plans. Americans, on the other hand, often forget to plan for different options and scenarios.

DEFEAT THE AFTERNOON DOLDRUMS

For many people, their energy tide begins to ebb about 3:00 o'clock in the afternoon. A few others may hit their low at another time of day. Try to identify your likely lull in energy and adopt some strategies to turn the tide.

A few suggestions include:

- Schedule people activities instead of paperwork at this hour.

- Go for a brisk walk up and down the stairs or around the building.

- Watch out for negative thought patterns that crop up when you're tired and instead give yourself positive messages.

- Work on a variety of less demanding tasks during low-energy periods and plan challenging projects that demand extended concentration for your high-energy hours.

OVERCOME PROCRASTINATION

True procrastinators don't want to think about procrastination as a problem. Most suffer the Scarlett O'Hara complex — I'll just think about it tomorrow. Since many people drag their feet on problem solving and analyzing, the tendency will be to skip this section or to think you'll come back to this part later. But the first step toward overcoming procrastination is admitting it's a problem. Procrastination is a habit, one that gets in the way of your success.

Determine Whether Procrastination Is Lowering Your Productivity

Executives who procrastinate create disorganization and confusion among their team members. The vice president of a textile company called on my firm to determine why his department was suffering from high turnover and low morale. The real culprit was his own procrastination, which caused subordinates to work late, frantically trying to meet deadlines and continually operating in a crisis mode. He thought he had lazy workers who lacked commitment when in fact his own poor time management skills were creating chaos.

If you find yourself berating the work ethic of your employees, then take notice. This is a danger signal that YOU may be the source of the problem. Consider whether procrastination is the culprit. Ask yourself these questions: Do I sit on information? Am I working longer and harder? Do my team members have to scramble most of the time to get their work done? Do I shoot the messengers who tell me to get on with it? Do I take time to listen to what my team members are suggesting? Does my procrastination affect others?

Substitute Real Work For Busy Work

Many executives fill their days with busy work that distracts their attention from the big issues facing the company. A small business with 50 years of successful operations under its belt was facing a decline in profits and productivity. The owner was ready to sell, when he called for help. Our analysis showed that he took his time doing everyday, routine tasks that could be delegated. As a result, he had no time to plan, sell services, organize or manage. He made no long-range strategies, but let one year just roll into the next. Was he busy? You bet! Was he effective? No way! He used busy work to avoid making decisions. This business owner failed to manage the growth of the industry or the decline of the economy because he had procrastinated on dealing with key financial and marketing issues.

Look at your week. Were you so busy doing routine activities that you failed to really mind the store, the direction of the store, the long- and short-range plans, and financial goals? If so, procrastination may be working, while you're just busy.

Identify Why You Procrastinate

You need to identify what type of activities you put off and why. Then see if you can find a creative solution. Look through your calendar or TO DO list and see what projects are carried forward from day to day. Do they have anything in common? Figure out what you can do to make the task easier or to motivate yourself to get it out of the way early.

For instance, suppose you dread composing a quarterly report because you dislike the number crunching involved. Every quarter you delay until the last moment before putting in a late night at the office to churn it out. Think about some alternatives. Maybe you could assign that portion of the report to a subordinate with a knack for numbers. Or perhaps the company computer whiz could design a program that would do the figuring automatically. Maybe the report could be eliminated altogether and never be missed. Or, you might schedule time to finish in your calendar and schedule a reward, contingent upon its completion.

Plan Rewards

Ultimately, there will always be some projects that tempt you to drag your feet and yet *must* be done. Planning a reward can help you get started and finished. Upon completing the task, reward yourself with something you really like to do. The reward can be simple and inexpensive. I like to listen to a motivational tape and give myself positive feedback. This type of reward is energizing, costs little, and creates an environment for success. Reading a good book or going out to dinner are other favorites of mine.

Consider The Positive Effects
Think about how finishing the dreaded activity will improve your day, further your goals, appease your boss, or help you sleep better that night. Visualize what it will feel like when you are finished. Whatever you do, don't let procrastination sneak in and steal your success.

USE PRE-SLEEP SUGGESTIONS
When I first heard about this technique, I thought it sounded like the *Twilight Zone*, but I gave it a chance. Pre-sleep suggestions are a form of positive thinking. At night, when you are lying in bed, relax and mentally visualize your next day. See yourself rising at a particular time, energized and refreshed. If you do this regularly, you will never need an alarm clock. Then visualize the next morning, with everybody leaving happily. Envision yourself at the office, with the people around you smiling and you smiling back. See things going smoothly in meetings and appointments. In this manner, you program yourself for success.

A "yes" face increases your chances for a "yes" day.

I frequently "see" meetings, conferences, phone calls and routine tasks going well. More often than not, things will happen as they are envisioned. This technique puts you in a positive frame of mind, what I call the *yes face*. Since you tend to get what you give, your positive outlook will elicit positive responses from others. Even if the day goes awry, I feel good enough to overcome the problems without undue anxiety.

Additionally, pre-sleep suggestions help you plan for the next day and generate alternatives for sticky situations. As with preparing for an interview, thinking through possible questions and obstacles can help you be prepared with your answers and presentation.

I was once asked to speak to an audience that had booed the previous year's speaker off the stage. The person who requested me to come was very honest about how "tough and difficult" this group can be. Instead of worrying and wringing my hands, I used pre-sleep suggestions to plan what I wanted to say, how I wanted to say it, and how to keep the group's attention and interest. When I met the group in Phoenix, we had a great time. It was one of the most responsive groups I've seen. A yes face, pre-sleep suggestions and good planning made the conference a positive situation.

CHOOSE OBJECTIVES RATHER THAN ACTIVITIES

Too often we jump into activities without prior reflection. Consider your objectives rather than just your TO DO list. Check to see if your activities reinforce your goals and priorities before committing to them. This perspective will eliminate many of the meetings, calls, appointments and projects that drain your time.

One of my associates, Sam, practices this technique. As a result, his meetings stay on focus and are productive. And he helps me stay on track, too. When I was invited to participate in a joint business venture recently, I was tempted to join. Sam asked me point-blank, "How does it fit in with your objectives?" In that light, I had to admit the venture would be a mistake for the company. By keeping objectives front and center, I avoided a major investment of time and dollars.

STICK TO YOUR ESTIMATES

Estimate how much time projects are worth and stick to your limits. Writers can understand this principle easily. A written document can always be improved, changing an adjective here or a verb there. But at some point, the author has to decide the piece is finished. Striving for perfection may be honorable, but it's rarely efficient. Don't work extra hours trying to perfect a project. Decide what the job is worth and complete it within the allocated time.

ELIMINATE THE EPITAPH

Get rid of the epitaph: *I Just Knew This Would Happen*. Do you spend large percentages of your time patching things that went wrong? Do you frequently despair in mid-project, seeing that your worst fears are coming to life and you'll be weeks behind deadline once again? People who think in this *I Just Knew This Would Happen* mode are victims of their own lack of planning. Learn to plan for the best and worst case scenario. Preparing for the worst can save you lots of time when an assignment does go off track. You'll be ready for the challenge and resolve problems more quickly.

LOOK OUT FOR COMPETITION

If you are a highly competitive person, stay away from other highly competitive people. These people add stress and tension to your day and unconsciously misdirect your energies. In a competitive environment, you tend to race in many different directions and take off in fruitless pursuits. In this driven frame of mind, you overlook planning, forgetting that the slow, steady, single-minded turtle most often wins the race.

PRACTICE POSITIVE THINKING

Think positively about yourself and your work. Few things can slow you down as quickly as feelings of inadequacy and inferiority. Since you are responsible for your own success or failure, cultivate positive thinking. Make a list of your strengths and refer to it regularly. Remind yourself of the talents you bring to your organization.

At my son's school one day I noticed a bulletin about Olympic athletes and how to become one. The first point was to think like a winner. This principle can be translated to the business world. Winners think like winners. Most successful executives think confidently.

TAKE ADVANTAGE OF COMMUTING

If you live 30 minutes from your office, you will likely spend 240 hours a year commuting. This "down time" can be productive. Play tapes, dictate letters and memos, rehearse speeches, or plan your day. A young executive in one of my client companies learned German in one year by simply playing tapes while he commuted. Later, when the company initiated relations with a German manufacturer, he was tapped to head the division.

How do you use your time commuting? On a train ride home from New York to Connecticut, you'll typically find three kinds of executives: those who work, those who whine and those who unwind. Some executives will write reports, legal briefs, books and otherwise use their time productively. Others never leave the bar, where they complain to one another about their dead-end jobs, inept bosses and crazy schedules. The third kind of commuter spends the trip relaxing by reading, writing or listening to tapes.

Commuting time can be productive.

There's no doubt which two types of executives arrive, ready to see their families and which type leaves the train feeling even further behind and impatient with the demands of their families. Don't make a hard day even harder by dwelling on the negatives, but use the time to turn the tide with positive steps.

An associate of mine tries to vary her commuting activities according to how the day has gone. If it has been a stressful, hard charging day, she'll listen to fiction on tape. If the day has been slow and she needs mental stimulation, she'll select informational or motivational tapes. The key, she says, is to know what you need, rather than doing the same activities day after day out of habit.

CONFIRM APPOINTMENTS

For appointments that are made far in advance, call the day before to confirm them. You'll save yourself time in preparation and travel to forgotten appointments. When meeting someone at the airport, call the airline before you leave and confirm the flight's arrival time. Many times, planes are late, and you can work a few minutes longer before heading to the airport.

SET UP CONTINGENCY PLANS

When working with another person, it pays to set up contingency plans — if a situation changes, you both can respond in concert. For instance, suppose you must fly to New York to coordinate a client meeting with a partner. You plan to handle the first portion of the presentation and your associate the second part, and you arrange to meet for coffee to go over the content at 10:00 a.m. Any number of things from flight problems to traffic could delay your arrival. To avoid panic and confusion, make a contingency plan the day before: If I fail to arrive by 10:30, go ahead to the meeting room, set up, and start with your portion of the presentation.

Surviving The
Paper Avalanche

The more paper clutters your desk, the easier it is to lose important items, materials, and thoughts. Most executives are buried under an avalanche of paper. This age of fax machines, desktop copiers and personal computers has produced an enormous amount of informational paperwork. Those business people who don't know how to handle the avalanche find themselves merely shuffling piles of papers around on their desks. And the situation only gets worse as it continues to snow.

Technology has yielded more paper and with it, more stress, more distractions, and more work.

The consequences of paper mismanagement are lost opportunities and increased stress. How often do you have to frantically search your desk for an important document? How many times a month do you miss an interesting seminar or luncheon because the flyer was buried in your in-basket? Is your backlog of reading material stacked higher than two inches?

When I enter someone's office, I can usually tell how productive that person is. Most of the time, people with just one folder on their desks accomplish more than other workers.

Because they are focused on one job, undistracted by paper clutter, they can give tasks their best shot. These executives control their work, rather than letting paper control their activities.

It's almost scary, though, to have a clean desk. The stacks of paper and publications can give you a sense of worth and value. You may harbor a hidden fear that if you got to the end of your paper trail, you'll have outgrown your usefulness to the company. And as long as there's paperwork to process, you know you'll never be twiddling your thumbs — you'll look busy, important and hopefully indispensable.

Eliminating clutter gives you more time to think and plan.

But failing to conquer paper clutter can cripple your ability to function effectively. Consultant Barbara Hemphill views paper clutter as "postponed decisions." You can't or won't decide what to do with a piece of paper, so you toss it in a pile to deal with it later. Eliminating those piles, however, will free you to work on priority projects and give you time to *think* on the job. It will also polish your image as someone who's responsive, organized and on top of things.

This chapter is divided into five major sections: Eliminating Paper Clutter, Filing, Dealing with Publications, Reading, and Writing. The tips that follow will help you get a handle on paper so that you function most effectively on the job. Many of these techniques can also be applied successfully at home.

PART ONE

ELIMINATING PAPER CLUTTER

The first step in managing paper is to get rid of the clutter. As you dig out from under the avalanche, you'll clear your desk and clear your mind at the same time.

USE YOUR CIRCULAR FILE

Man's best friend is not a dog. It's a file, a round file, a waste basket — the bigger, the better. Learn to use this circular file effectively.

Always sort your mail near a trash can. I don't even open junk mail, but toss it immediately. You can also throw envelopes and other nonessential papers directly into the trash before laying them down on your desk.

If you are hesitating with a paper in hand, Stephanie Winston, author of *The Organized Executive*, recommends playing the worst case scenario. Ask what will happen if you throw it out. Is this the only copy? Will you lose your job if you can't put your fingers on it? If not, go ahead and toss it. The company archives can reside in somebody else's office.

DIG OUT

A lawyer once hired my firm because he was missing deadlines and wanted help. The moment I stepped across his threshold, I saw the problem. Literally. Stacks of legal briefs, files and books teetered atop chairs, tables and window sills. The top rims of his glasses were barely visible above the stacks of files and papers on his desk. He was a living caricature of paper clutter.

His situation was an extreme case, but many executives do struggle with a paper overload. The first step to take toward better time management is to dig out from under all the paper. Piece by piece, papers and publications need to be sorted and processed until you reach ground zero. Then you can make a fresh start. This attorney spent two weeks digging out, and the investment in time and energy paid off immeasurably. His productivity increased, deadlines were met, and his life became manageable.

SORT YOUR PAPERS

Consider what you can do with a piece of paper other than leave it in a pile on your desk. You can *read* it, *delegate* it to another person, *act* on it, *file* it, or *trash* it. Make three file folders labeled ACTION, FILE, and READ. When digging out or processing incoming material, sort papers into one of these folders or throw them in the wastebasket or delegate them by putting them in a folder with someone's name on it. This procedure gets all those scattered, miscellaneous pieces of paper off your desk and into a system where you can control them. A few items go into a tickler file, which will be discussed later in this chapter.

CLEAR YOUR DESK BY QUADRANTS

If you are really buried, start digging out in sections. Draw an imaginary vertical line down the center of your desk and a horizontal line across the middle to create quadrants. Your next task is to clear each quadrant, one by one.

Dividing your desk this way will help keep you from simply rearranging or diverting papers to another section of the desk. Resist the temptation to move papers toward you or into one big pile. Concentrate on clearing one quadrant at a time. If necessary, schedule each quadrant on four consecutive days.

You'll need time and lots of trash bags. If you find small pieces of paper and loose jottings, put them in your ACTION file for now. Eventually, you can enter them in your card file, Rolodex, calendar or tickler file.

KEEP PAPERS OFF YOUR DESK

Make a sustained effort to keep papers off your desk. Some people promote only touching a piece of paper one time. I think this is unrealistic, but I do appreciate their idea. Try to sort papers immediately into their appropriate action folder to keep your desk area clear or at least sort them at the end of the day so you will start with a clean slate the next morning.

SCHEDULE A SUPER SATURDAY

If you have a large backlog of paperwork, the best time to process it is during a block of uninterrupted time. Since this time rarely occurs during a routine work day, consider holding a Super Saturday for yourself and your department heads. Ask everyone to come to the office during designated hours one Saturday with the goal in mind of plowing through paperwork. Give plenty of notice to avoid any hard feelings and tell them to dress casually. Have a catered lunch and give everyone a day off of their own choosing in exchange.

TEAM UP WITH YOUR SECRETARY
Enlist the aid of an assistant or secretary to divert paper trails from your office. With training, this person can route mail, answer routine correspondence, discard junk mail and file papers before you ever have to see them (See Pass Plays, Chapter 5).

DEVELOP A SORTING SYSTEM
Let your assistant sort your incoming papers into urgent and important folders. This helps eliminate paper clutter and helps you focus more quickly.

SYSTEMATIZE YOUR TELEPHONE NUMBERS
Many pieces of paper are kept for their valuable phone numbers. A large majority of business people use a Rolodex, a small, alphabetical desktop system. Whether you prefer this system, a notebook or a computer program for recording phone numbers, make sure you will have quick access to it.

Add frequently used numbers to a portable list that can go in your pocket or purse. Or use a copier to reduce it to a size that fits in your wallet. Also enter these numbers in the back of your calendar, so you'll always have them with you.

HIGHLIGHT TELEPHONE NUMBERS
Go through your Rolodex and highlight the telephone numbers on all your cards. And whenever you receive a business card, highlight the phone number before filing it in your Rolodex. This technique will save time scanning the cards to find a phone number. If using an electronic directory, put the phone numbers in bold type.

Also highlight numbers in the telephone book. This way, if you call again, the number is readily available. We have highlighters by all the telephone directories in our office.

ESTABLISH A PAPER LOCATION

At home and at work, designate a particular area, preferably with a telephone and trashcan in reach, as your location for processing the mail. Too often, we scatter our mail and waste time looking for it. Make sure your action folders, pens, paper, stamps, and whatever you will need to respond are nearby; it's easy to delay responding if you must get up and search for something.

PROCESS ROUTINE PAPERWORK ROUTINELY

If possible, set aside a daily time period for processing phone calls, letters and paperwork. You will be less likely to let routine paperwork pile up, and others will learn that you are unavailable at that time. Block the hours out on your calendar and have your secretary screen calls to make the time more productive.

CALENDARIZE YOUR PAPER CLUTTER

One way to help clear your desk is to record essential information in your calendar and throw the papers away. Suppose you receive a memo requesting your presence at a meeting. In your calendar, jot down the time, place and phone number and toss the memo. If you must keep the memo for some other information, file it and jot a file reference next to your calendar entry. This technique works well for conferences, invitations, meetings, and other appointments.

You can also use your calendar to jog your memory. For example, suppose you read in the newspaper about an upcoming business luncheon you'd like to attend. Make a calendar note on the day you should call for a reservation (with a phone number) and a note on the day of the luncheon (with time and location). Toss the newspaper article. When I liquidated a money market account recently by phone, I made a note in the middle of the next week that the check should have arrived. If it hadn't, the calendar entry would have prompted me to call my representative and track down the problem.

START A 3x5 CARD FILE

Battling those scribbled notes and scraps of paper that accumulate on your desk is easy with a 3x5 (or 5x7) card file. Use a box of these cards and index tabs with topical labels for organizing extraneous information. For instance on a card under the topic *Magazine Subscriptions*, enter the date you subscribe to a journal and when it expires. By referring to this card, I have noticed some magazines try to bill as much as two years in advance. It makes little sense to me to pay a subscription 18 months before it's due. I would rather use or invest my money for that period of time!

This card file is handy for all sorts of valuable information. Here are a few other topics I find particularly useful:

- *Catalog Orders*. I note what was ordered, when, and with whom I spoke. We had a disagreement at the office with an audio-visual company who billed us instead of our client. The company had trouble getting it straight, but we had the facts on our card. When returning their calls, I knew whom to ask for, the dates of previous conversations, and what had transpired during the calls.

- *Items Loaned*. My staff often lends video tapes, books, and audio tapes to clients as part of our ongoing work with them. We are glad to loan them, but we do want materials back. This card has saved the day when another client wants to borrow an item. If we don't have it, then we can easily find out who does. A friendly telephone call has the item in hand with no more wracking our brains trying to remember to whom we loaned it.

- *Membership Cards.* I support many different institutions, but dislike cluttering my wallet with their membership cards. Filing them behind this topic helps me keep track of the cards for those few days a year I need them.

- *Repair Persons.* I keep notes on whom I used and what kind of job they did. When friends or associates call for a suggestion or the copier breaks down again, I have a ready reference.

- *Safe Deposit Box.* List everything you keep in your safe deposit box for a sure reference when you can't remember. Use rubber cement to attach the key to the card, and you'll never have to search for it again.

- *Storage Items.* Number your boxes in the office storage closet or your attic at home and note their contents on this card. The next time you want the audit report from five years ago or Aunt Nellie's punch bowl, check the card for box numbers, instead of rummaging through entire storage areas.

- *Social Security Numbers.* I keep a listing of social security numbers for every member of my immediate family and direct employees. It is invaluable for completing the numerous forms that now require such identification.

- *Wallet Inventory.* List all the items you carry in your wallet, including credit cards with their account numbers. If it's ever stolen, you'll know exactly what needs replacing.

MAKE TRIP FILES

When you schedule a trip, make a file labeled according to your destination. Put papers related to this trip into the folder including your itinerary, tickets, notes of items to carry with you and passport. I also include a 3x5 card for each day, listing all the important times, people and places. This is a great way to keep up with confirmation numbers.

PART TWO

FILING

Filing is an essential part of clearing your desk. The key is to file only what you need to keep and to be able to find the items you've filed.

USE A TICKLER FILE

A tickler file is an essential organizing tool for office workers. It allows you to keep track of all sorts of information, gets paper off your desk and into a clear retrieval system.

To create a tickler file, label 12 file folders with the months of the year and order them with the upcoming month first. Next label 31 folders numerically to represent the days of the month. Put the numbered file folders at the front of your desk drawer, with all the monthly folders behind them. I keep my tickler file in the right hand drawer of my desk, in front of my alphabetical file, because I am in and out of it all day long.

A tickler file gets paper off your desk and into a clear retrieval system.

Suppose this is the month of April. Anything appropriate for April will be filed by day in the numbered folders. For instance, handouts for a meeting on April 21 go into file 21. Anything for future months goes in the appropriate monthly folder. Plane tickets for a June vacation will be stowed in the June file.

On the last work day of the month, take out next month's folder and empty that folder on your desk. Look at all the work that has accumulated for that month and organize it by days, 1-31. In other words, you are *tickling* that information throughout the month. If you have a project that will take six hours, then put a tickler for it behind each day of the month you plan to work on it. If you write a letter requesting a response in two weeks, put your copy of the letter 14 days ahead as a reminder.

In addition to tracking information over time, the tickler file simplifies your scheduling. Before leaving the office, consult your tickler file for the next day (see Chapter 1). The folder will contain a few items for your TO DO list and help you visualize your day.

ORDER YOUR REGULAR FILES

Use broad categories for your files and arrange them alphabetically. Hanging files are good for organizing these general categories. File papers in their most general file first. When it becomes bulky, you can break it down into subheadings using file folders.

For instance, you might now have files labeled Contracts, Financial Plans, Marketing Plans, Photo Releases, and Trade Agreements. These topics could be divided into two general categories: BUSINESS PLANS and LEGAL INFORMATION. In the first category, place folders labeled Financial and Marketing. Under the second category, place Contracts, Photo Releases and Trade Agreements.

CLEAN OUT CABINETS ANNUALLY

Clean out your filing cabinets annually. Research shows that you need to retain only 20 percent of the information placed in file drawers. When you run out of filing space, don't rush to buy a new cabinet. It's a signal to pare down your stored paperwork. Every year, my staff and I use the end-of-the-year holiday lull to clean out our file drawers.

ASSIGN DISCARD DATES

Before filing a document, put a discard date, in pencil, in the upper, right-hand corner. Later, when you go into your files and see something out of date, you can toss it without taking time to read it. Many people do clean out their files, but it takes them forever because they have to reread everything. Save yourself time by putting the discard date on *before* you file.

FILE BY TOPIC, NOT SOURCE

Many times we are tempted to file papers by their source, but try to file according to how a document will be used. For a long time, I kept a file labeled *Reader's Digest* Articles, containing articles I wanted to keep for their helpful information. The information was of no help, though, because I never opened the folder. Since reorganizing this file and sorting these articles by their topics, I use them frequently. For instance, an article on good salesmanship was moved to a Customer Service folder, where I can find it when I'm researching this topic.

STAPLE, DON'T CLIP

Paper clips make filing more tedious by catching on other documents. Papers can also get accidentally "clipped" to the wrong set and cause confusion. Papers that need to stay together should be stapled when possible. If papers can't be stapled, use the holding clips with springs. These clips prevent snagging.

FILE FROM BACK TO FRONT

Whenever you add to a file, put the papers on the top (or front) of a file. That way, your most recent information is easily visible and your oldest, more likely to need discarding, papers are at the back.

LABEL FILE DRAWERS

Label the outside of your file drawers either by letters of the alphabet (A-L, for example) or the subject matter contained within. You can go immediately to the right file drawer when searching for a document.

LABEL PAPERS BY FILE

Before putting a document in your FILE folder, decide where it should be filed. Jot the file location in the upper right-hand corner of the top page, along with the discard date. Then whoever files the document will put it where you can find it again and won't have to take time to read the material to determine where it goes. And you'll be able to find it again if your assistant is away from the office.

RENT A SAFE DEPOSIT BOX

Important or irreplaceable documents should be kept in a safe deposit box or fireproof, locked safe. You might keep a listing of your safe deposit box contents in your 3x5 card file or a designated file.

I copy key computer files onto diskettes and store them in a safe place away from the office. In case of disaster, I'll have duplicates of my most important files. If the material is changed frequently, such as text for a book in progress or accounts receivable information, remember to update these stored files regularly.

PART THREE

DEALING WITH PUBLICATIONS

One of the questions I'm asked most frequently is how to deal with publications. From *The Wall Street Journal* to trade magazines, reading is a vital part of an executive's job. Here are a few tips to help you stay in the know, while keeping those stacks at a manageable level.

TOSS OLD MAGAZINES

Every year on our family beach trip, my sister hauls along a box of magazines. At the end of the week she hauls it home again, without having read a single publication. She is always sure the vacation will give her time to read all the articles she has saved from a year's worth of subscriptions.

Forget all those old magazines. If they are more than three months old, toss them in the recycling bin. And don't feel guilty about it — most of us try to read more than is necessary anyway. A good executive needs to stay in touch, but can easily overdo it with publications.

REDUCE YOUR NUMBER OF SUBSCRIPTIONS

Inventory your magazines and decide which ones are important to you personally and professionally. Cancel your subscriptions for all the other ones. If you are not reading a magazine, why pay for it?

DE-CIRCULATE YOUR NAME

Take your name off the office circulation lists for publications that hold little interest. And call or write the subscription offices of complimentary magazines and newsletters that you receive and never read and have your name deleted. You'll save time, and they'll save postage.

RIP AND READ

Rather than flipping through a magazine for interesting articles, review the table of contents. Decide which articles you want and tear them out. Put only the "ripped" articles in your READ folder and throw out the magazine. You'll save time skimming advertisements and reading articles that snare you with a well-written lead or photograph.

SKIM HEADLINES

Learn to read a newspaper by its headlines. Then read only the articles that interest you or tear them out for your READ folder.

USE A READ FOLDER

Anything that can be read in 10 to 15 minutes should go in your READ file. Take this folder everywhere. It comes in handy for inopportune moments of waiting. Whether you are backed up on the Interstate, in line for airline tickets, or sitting through a half-time show, you can catch up on reading while you wait.

CONQUER CATALOGS

How many catalogs have you kept because you liked an item in it, but weren't ready to pull out your credit card and order it? How many times have you searched through a stack of catalogs to find that one item you wanted, but couldn't remember which company offered it? With the boom in direct mail during the last decade, most households and offices are overflowing with catalogs.

Try tearing out the pages of interest and throwing the rest away - just make sure the phone number for ordering appears. Or, when you see something you like, write the item name and page number on the front cover of the catalog or mark it with a self-adhesive note. This way you can flip immediately to the item without reviewing the entire catalogue. If you can't find anything you'd like to order, throw it away.

WEED YOUR BOOKSHELVES

If you are tight on shelf space or reading time, don't feel guilty about getting rid of some books. You can give them away to colleagues, donate to a library, school, or professional association or sell them at a secondhand bookstore.

PART FOUR

READING

Reading is one of the first tasks to be cut when time is tight. Phone calls, letters, presentations and other jobs call out for attention. Your reading material — reports, publications, research, and the like — sits quietly and waits. But don't underestimate the importance of your reading. Keeping up with it helps you know your industry and better understand your company. It keeps you looking ahead, when other tasks might bog you down. Rule Number One is to set aside time for reading.

SCHEDULE TIME FOR READING

The only way you will ever get all your reading done is to schedule time for it. If it is important to you, block out the time on your calendar and ask your secretary to hold calls. I try to schedule three 20-minute blocks per week for reading. I would probably never find a full hour, but three sessions keeps me on track. At my company, we also schedule regular READ-INs, usually on a Friday. On those days, instead of going out to lunch, everyone uses that time catch up on reading.

CIRCULATE MATERIAL BEFORE READING IT

Before reading informational documents or publications, circulate the material among your managers. Ask them to mark important items by highlighting them and add their input. When the material returns, you can absorb it quickly by reading the highlights. This tip can save you hours of reading. If needed, you can assign people different colors if you want to track differences of opinion.

HAVE ASSISTANTS PREVIEW YOUR READING

Your assistant or secretary can also read lengthy material and underscore important points, particularly any requests and deadlines, and attach information you will need for making a decision. This system allows you to make an immediate response rather than setting the document aside until you have time to obtain the necessary backup information or time to read it in detail.

SPEED READ

Learn to speed read. A vast amount of the paper that crosses your desk is insignificant. From junk mail to interoffice memos, most paperwork has little impact on your work. Speed reading classes teach you to read for critical points and key information. Watch out for those few items, however, that will still need to be read in detail.

I have recommended that entire executive offices learn speed reading. Bring in an instructor every Friday for a month and track the difference it makes. Another option is to investigate computer programs designed to increase your reading speed and comprehension.

LIMIT FYI MATERIAL

Let colleagues and subordinates know you only wish to receive critical material and try to avoid FYI memos. Many executives lose time skimming through nonessential publications and reports that are sent under the "For Your Information" banner.

REQUIRE RECOMMENDATIONS

Establish a policy for requiring subordinates to include their recommendations for any problems they send for your review. Sometimes employees hope to dodge problems by passing the decision upward. Asking for their recommendation forces them to thoroughly analyze a problem before sending it your way. And, if their ideas are strong, your job is often reduced to a stamp of approval.

REQUIRE COVER PAGES

Require reports longer than three pages to include a cover page. This page should state the report's objective, a summary of data, its conclusions and recommendations. This procedure forces your subordinate to think cogently.

EVALUATE ROUTINE REPORTS

Inventory all the regular reports generated by your department. Go through them and determine which can be eliminated, which could be combined, which can be shortened and which ones should continue as they are. Then make the changes. You and your department will save time preparing and reading reports that may have outlived their usefulness.

A division of one of my client companies decided to

evaluate the priority of each routine report in an effort to reduce paperwork. At last count, this division had eliminated 42 reports, giving them 1,082 hours of productive time!

PART FIVE

WRITING

Along with public speaking, writing may well be one of the most dreaded tasks for executives. Years can go by between composing your last college term paper and facing your first big writing assignment on the job. A few techniques can make stringing words together a little less worrisome.

BUY A LAPTOP

Laptop computers offer users a great way to churn out work while on the go. A national talk radio host takes a laptop on board planes and answers his electronic mail while flying. I've seen doctors conducting their research on laptops while they wait in hospital lounges and conference rooms. And during a recent convention, two of every ten executives took notes on their laptop computers. It sure beats taking notes by hand and later putting them into your computer.

A laptop computer makes "down" time productive.

The new notebook computers are smaller than laptops and provide an efficient way to travel and maintain your paperwork. On a recent three-week business trip, I easily carried one of these computers, a portable fax and mobile telephone. My office was literally transportable as I visited cities across the country.

These situations are all good uses of modern technology, and many more opportunities await the alert executive. When traveling, select a hotel and airline that will accommodate your technological needs.

MAKE MARGIN NOTES

Write your responses to correspondence on the letter as you read. Your secretary can prepare it in formal style and save you the time writing out or dictating the recipient's name, company, address, phone number and subject references. This also helps prevent spelling errors. In some circumstances, you can return the letter with your notes on it — a surefire way to get their attention.

IDENTIFY YOUR NEXT STEPS

When leaving a project in midstream, write a note outlining your next step or steps. Insert this note at the top of the folder. When you are ready to start again, you will know exactly where you left off and what you need to do. This saves you 15 to 20 minutes of getting back into the project before you actually start working.

USE MIND MAPPING

Mind mapping is an organizing technique, similar to diagramming sentences. It works for articles, presentations, letters, speeches and other lengthy writing projects. Before beginning a project, write down in fewer than three words your main topic and circle it. Then think about the major points you'd like to make and draw "spokes" around the circle with one point per spoke. Beside each point, list related ideas that should be covered. Outlining a writing assignment this way organizes your thoughts and helps give your finished product clarity and completeness.

CREATE MACROS AND FORM LETTERS

Macros are gifts; use them well and frequently. Computer macros are files that consist of a sequence of keystrokes, recorded so that they can be used repeatedly. They may contain text or commands such as the formatting codes of a document. If you or your secretary use a computer frequently, macros can be big time savers. Develop forms for common correspondence and create the appropriate macros. Then you can delegate correspondence easily if your assistant is familiar with the material. All that needs to be added is a salutation and any information unique to a specific letter.

LEARN YOUR COMPUTER'S CAPABILITIES

Much of the popularity of the personal computer can be attributed to its time-saving capabilities. Running spreadsheets and word processing are two of the most popular functions for which computers save an individual hours of time. Learn the capabilities of your computer and put them into practice.

Computer fluency can be an asset.

An executive once told me he didn't need to be bothered with learning to use a computer — his assistant took care of all his computer work and word processing. A few months later I saw him in the San Diego airport. He laughed when I asked how things were going.

His former company had been purchased and downsized, putting him out of work. He took some computer classes to fill his time between jobs. His new job is great, but that company also downsized, leaving one assistant for every six vice presidents. These executives are required to type their own computer memos, because it saves time for everyone. His computer skills helped him adapt.

I recently consulted with another company that has pared down to one assistant for every 27 managers. In the age of downsizing, it is fatal to assume someone will always be there to do your routine work.

PREPRINT POSTCARDS

Consider preprinting small cards for repetitive correspondence. If you frequently send information at the request of a client, you may benefit from attaching a card, preprinted with your company logo, your name and a notation such as "Enclosed is the information you requested."

For sending inter-office material, you might preprint a

postcard with your name and a selection of boxes to be checked as follows:

☐ For your information.
☐ Please handle.
☐ Let's discuss.
☐ Please read and return.
☐ Keep on file.

TAKE BREAKS

If faced with a big writing project, break it down into segments and work on it on different days. Set yourself a series of deadlines, one for each segment, rather than just a final deadline. You'll tend to write more quickly under short-term deadlines. If struggling to get something on paper, sleep on it. A good night's sleep can bring you fresh perspective and keep your writing from becoming flat.

RESIST WRITING HOLIDAY CARDS

Avoid sending end-of-the-year holiday cards. The task takes time, which is already scarce during the busy season. And, chances are, your correspondence will receive little attention amid the piles of cards most business people receive. Instead, consider sending cards for another holiday or special event such as St. Patrick's Day or Thanksgiving. Your message will stand out and have a greater impact than the traditional Christmas and New Year correspondence.

TAMING THE
MEETING LION

Meetings are notorious time wasters. Managers consistently report that at least half their meeting time is wasted. And when up to a third of the typical executive's day is spent in meetings, that's a lot of wasted time. In dollars and cents, an executive earning $50,000, who averages three hours per day in meetings, costs his company more than $10,000 annually in nonproductive time.

I have consulted with several companies lately where meetings are a status symbol. No longer is status determined by your model car or your neighborhood, but it's the number of meetings attended. The same man who told me how many

**Cutting down meeting time is a
quick route to greater productivity.**

meetings he attended also told me he arrived at 7 a.m. and left at 9 p.m. Although he was proud of this record, the burden was taking its toll on his health, his family and his employees. As one of five directors of a Fortune 500 company, he was setting an exhausting standard for the rest of his staff.

When you are in meetings all day, you fail to get your work done or you must work late in order to accomplish your goals. One of the quickest ways to cut down your work hours is to limit the amount of time spent in meetings.

An added benefit for the talented meeting leader is earning the respect of your colleagues and employees. A leader who starts late and lets meetings run too long will lose points with participants. On the other hand, an effective, focused leader will be appreciated.

When meetings are out of control, there are ways to tame them. You can shorten meetings by using some simple techniques.

PREPARE A WRITTEN AGENDA

Think of yourself as the facilitator of the meeting, the gatekeeper of conversation. You must control and direct the discussion. One way to stay on track is to develop an agenda. A printed agenda gives participants a focal point for discussion and gives you a reference point if discussion veers off track.

A good agenda:

- States a purpose for the meeting.

- Lists specific items to be covered.

- Allots a set amount of time for each item.

If applicable, contact participants ahead of time to see if they have items for the agenda. State a purpose for the meeting at the top of the agenda and distribute copies ahead of time. Pre-circulating an agenda that lists specific topics gives participants an opportunity to prepare for discussion and bring relevant materials to the meeting. Most people will bring their agendas to the meeting, but you should have extras on hand. You may want to post or project a large version on the wall or a screen for easy reference.

INVITE THE RIGHT PEOPLE — ONLY

Be sure the right people are invited and can attend. Many meetings are a waste of time when appropriate decision makers are absent. If someone with key information cannot attend, reschedule the meeting.

Research has shown that groups of 8 or fewer people work more effectively than larger groups. Invite only essential participants. Those employees who need to know information but have little input to offer can be updated later by memo or a copy of the minutes. If you must include a large number of people, consider assigning names in addition to allotted times on the agenda and allow participants to come and go as they are needed for certain items.

START ON TIME

In many corporations, meetings typically start 15 to 20 minutes after their appointed time. Even punctual employees, realizing this unspoken policy, will begin to arrive "late." If you start your meetings on time, failing to reward latecomers by waiting for them or reviewing the material they missed, participants will soon catch on. You also might try an unusual start time — 9:10 or 4:17 — to encourage others to arrive promptly.

END ON TIME

Put an end time as well as a start time on the agenda and make every effort to meet it. When an end time is stated, you can prompt participants by saying something like, "If we're going to get out of here by 2:00, we'll have to move along." And holding meetings just before lunch or quitting time practically guarantees a speedy conclusion.

USE A DEVIL'S ADVOCATE

You may be familiar with parking lot meetings, the unofficial gripe sessions that frequently follow an important meeting. Some participants, silent lions unwilling to air criticisms during a meeting, will roar later. Not only do these informal gatherings waste time, but they also sabotage company morale and delay accomplishing your goals. Appointing a devil's advocate sidesteps these lions. Pre-assign someone or ask for a volunteer to voice the negatives of an idea or proposal. When the group feels free to state objections, you are more likely to adopt a conclusion that has everyone's support.

TRY GROUP FACILITATION

Another way to lay concerns on the table is to divide participants into groups of four or five. Ask each group to come up with a key question or concern for the presenter. This way, participants can state their criticisms with some measure of anonymity. By encouraging group members to look at the downside rather than simply nodding their affirmation, you get better results and better cooperation in the long run.

PROMOTE A BUSINESS-LIKE ATMOSPHERE

One of my clients, an international manufacturing company, allows employees at all levels to dress casually. Jeans and polo shirts are the norm. But this casual look belies their mental attitudes. They come to meetings prepared and ready to work. The key to their productivity is the company culture established by executives who promote and expect a business-like atmosphere.

Your body language helps set the tone for business.

You set the stage for business through stated expectations and your own example. Let everyone know that they should be on time and be prepared. Tell them what they need to bring — last month's budget report or Bob's memo on European sales. Distribute an agenda and stick to it. Tolerate little, if any, chatter and discourage food and smoking. Pay attention to the messages you send through your body language. Speak in crisp energetic tones. Look others in the eye and sit up straight or lean forward in your chair.

CONDUCT STAND-UP MEETINGS

If you have a brief objective, meet in a corridor or room without chairs or ask the group to remain standing. You'll find that people think more quickly on their feet than in a comfortable chair. This technique works best for meetings of 20 minutes or less.

PLAN YOUR PRESENTATION

A little time in preparation saves a lot of time in the conference room. Define problems and identify possible solutions ahead of time. Have hand-out and audio-visual materials ready to go. On your agenda, you can jot down the points you want to make so that important ideas are not forgotten.

If you are making a presentation, remember that everyone is tuned to station WIIFM: *What's In It For Me?* State your ideas in terms of their benefits to the company and to individuals. Until the benefits are clear, others will be slow to rally in support of your ideas.

EVALUATE YOUR REGULAR MEETINGS

How many times has your weekly staff or team meeting been more like a social hour than a business update? How many companies hold team meetings every Monday morning? Thousands of companies are losing thousands of dollars through weekly departmental meetings that have lost sight of their business objectives.

Take time to evaluate your regularly scheduled meetings. Could weekly meetings be held monthly or monthly meetings held quarterly? If you're scheduling individual meetings with staff members, perhaps a group meeting would suffice. Define a purpose for these meetings to ensure that they are focused and meaningful.

DISCOURAGE LATE ARRIVERS

Some people are chronically late, and you may need to take stronger measures than simply starting on time and ignoring their behavior. For repeat offenders, make it clear to them outside of meetings that they are expected to be on time. If the problem persists, be creative. Give late participants an egg to hold throughout the meeting. Collect agenda items at the top of the meeting and refuse any late additions. Assign stragglers the task of taking minutes. Or, ask the team members what they think should be done.

One of my clients likes to move extra chairs away from the

conference table at the start of a meeting and put them against the walls. Latecomers find they must sit outside the inner circle of punctual participants.

REDUCE CHITCHAT
As with discouraging late arrivals, you can be creative in stifling the chitchat and comments that disrupt a meeting. One division of an international office equipment company was having trouble with their Monday morning sales meetings going off track. The manager initiated a "rule" that anyone who makes a distracting comment during the meeting must throw a dollar in the Fun Pot. When enough money is collected, the fund is used to buy a special treat for the team.

COVER BIG ISSUES EARLY
Let people warm up in a meeting by scheduling one or two noncontroversial items first. Then move on to the big issues while people are still fresh. If you wait too long to introduce a major topic, you may run out of time for needed discussion. And participants with an eye on the clock are more likely to simply approve an idea without giving it much thought.

HOLD MEETINGS IN SOMEONE ELSE'S OFFICE
It's easier to end and exit a meeting that's held in someone else's office. You can lead people to a close with comments like, "I know Roger has to get back to work, so let's wrap this up." You can also make a quick exit and avoid those participants who like to linger after the meeting to socialize or to have a few private words with the boss.

COMMUNICATE ON PAPER
For many people, calling a meeting is a reflex. A problem arises, and they immediately respond, "Maybe we should get together and discuss this." At first glance, a meeting appears the quick path to resolution. But, more often than not, you lose time in the long run.

    The best way to cut down on meeting time is to avoid

meetings altogether. Try "meeting" on paper by sending a memo or posting information. Another alternative is to use a check-off system in which you circulate material to a list of people with your name last. As it travels down the line, individuals can jot down their comments and check off their names. By the time the document returns to your desk, everyone will have had some input.

TAKE ADVANTAGE OF TECHNOLOGY

Technology provides plenty of alternatives to meetings. Many times, using fax machines, voice mail, electronic mail and telephone conferences can replace face-to-face meetings. Video conferences, if you have the capability, can save you travel time and speed proceedings. Most people won't bother with small talk when the camera is rolling. And they'll make their points more quickly.

Training your staff to use this technical equipment will yield long-term savings. Don't let machines intimidate you — they are great time savers. I work with many companies that have installed intricate voice mail systems that no one uses, because they don't know how. And just as often, I find that support staff can use the system, but managers and executives, who could benefit the most, rarely learn.

SEND SOMEONE ELSE

If your presence is not essential, send someone else. Your representative can take notes, speak for you, and afterwards summarize significant news or decisions. Don't underestimate the value of delegation.

PASS PLAYS

Management gurus all have particular ideas about what it takes to be a true leader. Although their philosophies differ in many ways, they generally agree that an effective leader is a team player.

Like a good coach, a true leader sets forth goals and makes everyone feel like a contributing player. Whether striving for a division championship or the Malcolm Baldridge Quality Award, great leaders propound a vision that inspires their team. And once inspired, the team members are given an opportunity to play and score.

Perhaps the most overlooked way to challenge your work force, and at the same time lighten your workload, is delegation. I once conducted a needs assessment survey, requested by the senior vice president of a Fortune 500 company. The results showed that his senior managers felt overworked and stressed. Their direct reports, on the other hand, complained that they wanted more challenging work. Increasing and improving delegation solved both problems.

**Delegating work challenges your employees
and frees you to concentrate on global issues.**

Many executives are reluctant to delegate for a number of reasons. For one, they believe they can do the work faster and better than anyone else. And they're usually right. After all, their performance is part of the reason they have risen to the top ranks.

For those with a crammed schedule, the time investment required makes little sense. Why spend three hours showing Bill how to configure the quarterly report when you can knock it out in less than an hour? It's easier and seemingly faster to say, "I'll just get this out of the way." This rationale for hanging on to work is a common one, but it's also short-sighted.

Another obstacle that may need to be overcome is a psychological one. Trust and self-confidence play large roles in an executive's reluctance to delegate. It's a form of turf war in which a manager feels threatened by ambitious employees. In giving away too much land, you think you'll ultimately jeopardize your kingdom.

Leaders view their workers as teammates.

Managers need to think of their employees as a team. Those assistants, hungry for bigger projects, are not threats — they are liberators. Delegating work, in an appropriate manner, frees you to be more productive and effective in your own work. It will give you time to think, plan, and direct operations, rather than entangling you in daily affairs. And the result will be an increase in productivity for the entire department, a positive reflection on you.

Employees who are motivated and challenged in their work aren't likely to instigate a coup or jump ship. Most will treasure a boss who seeks to develop them professionally and give them opportunities for advancement. Power plays generally come from frustrated employees who believe their boss is blocking their growth and ability to achieve. This chapter will examine leadership, how to delegate effectively and how to motivate your team. Once you learn the pass plays, you'll find you can go the length of the field much faster than before.

LEARN HOW TO DELEGATE

Many managers contend that delegated work is never performed properly or never comes back the way they wanted. Instead of faulting employees, these managers should look at their methods of delegation. To delegate effectively, you must be clear about the tasks at hand and explain exactly what results are expected. Let the employee know whether you'd like to make the final decision, merely review results or have no input at all.

Choose the Right Person

When delegating a task or project, make sure the employee is capable of doing the job. If you select someone with little or no experience in a relevant area, train them. Otherwise the results will be a frustrated or overwhelmed employee and work left undone.

An administrative assistant once told me she had been assigned a job to be done in Lotus. Because she was unfamiliar with the software, she couldn't do the work. Her boss failed to ask beforehand who in the office knew Lotus, but arbitrarily assigned the task to her. A more effective procedure would have been finding out who knew Lotus or asking the assistant if she could handle the job. Then she could have told him she didn't know Lotus, and the manager could have given the task to someone else or provided training.

Know Your People

If you don't know your employees well, consider surveying them informally to find out what interests them and where they think their talents lie. Ask them where they want to be in two years or five years. And study their records and resumes to understand their experience and backgrounds. When something comes along that you want to delegate, you'll have a better idea of who would be receptive to doing it and who would be qualified.

Assign the Authority

Be careful to assign a job to someone with the authority to execute it. A common mistake in delegation is to assign work to an assistant who lacks the power to make decisions or implement the procedures necessary for completing the job. It may seem logical to you that the authority goes with the assignment. But the employee and others on the team may need it spelled out. For their benefit, go ahead and state what new authority you are giving.

Find A Willing Employee

When making an assignment, question an employee as to his or her willingness to take on a new task. Make sure the worker is motivated and ready to accept the extra work. Simply dropping work on an unsuspecting subordinate can cause hard feelings. Being sensitive to circumstances can earn you big points with the team. And if you express your confidence in their ability to handle the new tasks, you'll find you are rarely turned down.

State When A Job Is Due

Stating a deadline for performance is critical to successful delegation. Be as specific as possible. Employees become frustrated with open-ended assignments, wondering how much priority to give them, and frustrated with you when asked where it is. Try giving *white lie* deadlines, dates a little earlier than the last minute. Then, if anything goes off track, you have time to regroup and revise.

Maintain Control

When you manage through others, keep control by holding subordinates responsible for their actions and checking the results of those actions. Try to strike a balance between stifling their initiative and losing control or knowledge of what's going on. From the outset, establish a system for feedback. It could be as simple as weekly memos reporting their progress or a scheduled meeting midway through the project.

Keep In Mind The Six Levels Of Delegation

Remembering the six levels of delegation will help you clarify your instructions for employees. Too often we say one thing when we really mean another. Delegation can be broken down as follows:

- Level I   Ask an assistant to obtain information — do the research and bring the information back to you for a decision.

- Level II   Ask an assistant to do research and make a recommendation.

- Level III   Ask an assistant to do research, obtain your decision and then follow through.

- Level IV   Ask an assistant to do the research, make a decision and implement it, with your approval.

- Level V   Ask an assistant to do a job and tell you when it is completed.

- Level VI   Just tell an assistant to do a job.

Too often we tell someone to take care of something, which is Level VI, when in reality we mean Level II: do the research and let me decide.

Offer Support

Offer encouragement to employees when handing out a task. Express your confidence in them and tell them you will be available for questions. Delegating work gives you a prime opportunity to boost the self-esteem of your workers.

Remember to provide the resources needed to complete a task. Think ahead so they won't have to return for help. Will Marilyn need last year's marketing plan or a slide projector or the name of a contact person in Accounting? Have these items ready when you make the assignment.

Make Fewer Decisions

Some assertive people like to take responsibility for all decisions. But making decisions is time consuming. Think about the kinds of things that require your input and consider who else could handle them. I always liked scheduling my own appointments. Now I have delegated most of this type of scheduling to an assistant. My time is free for other things, while my staff decides who, when and what.

Block Upward Delegation

Don't let subordinates delegate their problems to you. As an experienced, knowledgeable person, you may see easy solutions to their struggles. And you may be flattered by their faith in you. But make it clear that they need to think carefully before coming to you. Request written recommendations or analysis for any problems they want to discuss. That way, you are sure they have given the task some effort.

Also beware of allowing delegated tasks to return home. When an employee is struggling to learn a task and badgering you with questions, you may be tempted to take it over again — defeating your original purpose. Be as helpful as possible, but let them learn, even if it's the hard way.

SET AN EXAMPLE

Effective leaders must set an example for others. They must be self-managed, working and performing in the manner they expect from those around them.

That means:

- Be a model of good work habits and thinking patterns.

- Incorporate your goals into all activities. Focus on doing the right things, not just doing things right.

- Roll up your shirtsleeves and communicate with others at their levels. Walk the halls when you get a chance, instead of staying behind closed doors all day.

MAKE YOUR ADMINISTRATIVE ASSISTANT PART OF THE TEAM

Most executives require some basic functions from their assistants including typing, answering phones, taking dictation, and filing. In this regard, they act entirely on your instruction, taking little or no independent action. Take a closer look and you may discover some hidden abilities that can make your life easier.

Many assistants are capable of handling tasks requiring independent judgment such as screening the mail, tossing junk mail, handling some inquiries, making appointments, and tracking the progress of assignments. A few can do even more. These "super" assistants can compose letters, schedule appointments, keep your calendar, summarize reports, highlight reading material, and supervise junior clerical employees.

TRAIN YOUR EMPLOYEES

Provide some structured training. Too often employees who are given new assignments or promoted to a new position receive no formal training. They are expected to learn from other workers or the worker they replaced or rely on their own cleverness. In most companies, it's a sink or swim situation. Training your workers will save time and turmoil. Companies that emphasize training show better returns and higher earnings. Their training programs improve quality, lower costs and create an atmosphere of excellence.

EDUCATE WORKERS

If employees believe the company or the boss is genuinely concerned for their development and advancement, they will work harder and be more loyal than their counterparts at other companies. What better way to express your concern and invest in the future than to provide job-related education? Training is too often viewed as an unnecessary expense. But not only does it boost morale, it also increases the competence of your workers.

The CEO of a corporation asked me to evaluate a project that had cost the company $5 million. At the root of the problem was a lack of commitment to education. A cost-conscious manager had rejected a junior executive's request to attend a seminar where he would have learned new formulas for cost projections in marketing products — formulas that would have saved the company the expensive error. Whether it's learning cost projections or simply learning to read, invest in the future by investing in the education of your staff.

PLAN FOR RECOGNITION

Plan how to give recognition to your workers. Recognition keeps people motivated, but often busy executives forget how to honor their employees' accomplishments. Monetary bonuses are common awards, but you can be creative. One broadcasting company executive awards designated, prime parking spaces on a monthly basis to workers, who are nominated by peers and selected by managers.

INFORM YOUR STAFF

Discussing your priorities, vision and goals with your staff helps keep them motivated and makes them feel a part of the team. It reassures them that they are more than just pawns on the chess board. In addition, such communication helps them make smarter decisions and distinguish between busy work and real work. Your entire department will work more effectively when they are focused on the finish line.

USE FREELANCERS AND CONTRACTORS

Temporary services can fill your short-term needs for word processing and data entry. But they may be unable to help with complicated, in-depth projects. Consider hiring out special projects to a freelancer or contractor. The savings in time and anxiety can be well worth the cost. Many cities have networks of freelancers that, once you tap into them, will provide a goldmine of resources. And most cities have an abundance of independent contractors.

Writers, photographers, graphic artists, accountants, trainers, and various types of consultants can make life easier by knocking out your specialized projects in a professional manner. Before hiring, ask for and check references and review their portfolios. When assigning tasks, be sure to provide clear directions, any needed information and access to resources and people.

Dealing
With People

Communication skills are among the most sought-after traits in new hires. From their resumes to applications to interviews, job candidates are judged for their ability to understand and disseminate information. Corporate recruiters have good reason for scrutinizing these qualifications. Communication is an essential element of any job. And the higher your level of employment, the more critical the need for good communication skills.

Executives, especially those who manage large numbers of people, must have good interpersonal skills to be successful. Whether you initiate a conversation or not, whether sending or receiving information, you will benefit from learning techniques that make your interactions focused and productive. And learning to deal with interruptions is one of the most valuable people skills you can develop.

On average, managers are interrupted every eight minutes.

Statistics regarding the number of interruptions a typical manager faces in a day vary widely — from bad to worse. One expert gives an estimate as high as 140 times per day. A *U.S. News & World Report* article notes that the average manager is interrupted every eight minutes, which computes to 60 to 90 times per business day.

Whatever your actual number, dealing with interruptions is unavoidable. And it drains your productivity. Research has shown that once you are interrupted, it can take as long as 20 minutes to get reoriented to your work. If this figure were the case for just ten interruptions in a day, you could lose more than three hours of work.

Obviously the key to managing interruptions is to limit the number and reduce their length. You need to hone your people skills. To be effective, you need to season your commitment to productivity with diplomacy. You can start by incorporating the following pointers into your daily routine.

MAINTAIN A LOG OF INTERRUPTIONS

Try to catalog the types of interruptions you handle in a day. Such a log will help pinpoint problem areas. Depending on your job and environment, you may notice telephone calls account for 75 percent of your interruptions. Or perhaps you are barraged by drop-in visitors, a common problem for managers in high-tech fields. It may be your administrative assistant taking full advantage of your open-door policy. Once you identify the problem, finding solutions will be easier.

INSTITUTE T.E.A. TIME

Indispensable as it is, the telephone wastes time. It is particularly troublesome for extroverts, those who like to be with or talk with others. Use a T.E.A. formula to reduce the length of the phone calls you make:

- Tell the person why you called.
- Explain what you want them to do.
- Ask for action.

Following this plan eliminates chitchat that can add minutes to your call. Chances are good the other person will appreciate a short call as much as you do.

TAKE CONTROL OF CONVERSATIONS AT THE START

When handling incoming calls, never ask, "How are you?" unless you really want to know. Begin with "How can I help you?" This question focuses the call's purpose and gets to the issue. It also gives you control of the conversation from the beginning.

SCREEN CALLS

Reserve your immediate attention for important calls and screen out unnecessary ones. Ask your secretary to hold calls or use an answering machine or other voice system. Then you can return calls at your convenience.

GROUP PHONE CALLS

Returning phone calls in a group instead of one or two at a time will help you conduct them in a brisk, businesslike fashion. Let non-urgent messages collect over a period of time, then devote a block of time to going through the pile.

Doctors, by necessity, are experts at efficient phone use. Unable to leave exam rooms or conferences to take calls, they return them at set times during the day — usually lunch time or in the evenings before heading home. You, too, can guard your time like a doctor.

INSTALL ELECTRONIC MAIL

Installing electronic or voice mail throughout the company will allow everyone some uninterrupted work time. The systems record messages, as specific as they need to be. You can then return the calls in a group at your convenience. New technology allows messages to be picked up from a remote location so that you can access your messages day or night and process them during "down time."

These systems have a distinct advantage over having an assistant take messages. Unsure if or how a long message will be translated, many callers are reluctant to give assistants more than just a request to have the boss return their call. With electronic or voice mail, people generally leave messages as though they were speaking directly to you, giving more details and sometimes eliminating the need for a call back.

As a word of caution, however, I recommend that electronic mail be used with a large dose of common sense. It's great for internal communications, but when you deal with consumers or clients, be careful. If not used appropriately, voice mail can damage your public relations. The last thing clients want is to play telephone tag with a machine. If away from your desk for long periods of time, make sure someone covers your messages and returns calls.

BUY AN EGG TIMER FOR THE OFFICE

A three-minute egg timer helps you track how long you spend on a phone conversation. Every time you answer the telephone, turn it over and try to hang up before the sand runs out. Make a game of trying to beat the clock. If nothing else, it will make you conscious of your phone time.

SIGNAL THE CLOSE OF A CALL

We all know someone who seems to chatter endlessly about minor items. Your language can signal the end of a call. Say outright, "I really need to go." Or use conversation closers like, "Thanks for calling. I've enjoyed talking with you." Or, if appropriate, refer to an upcoming opportunity for further discussion such as, "Hope to see you Thursday at our meeting." Having a few phrases in your mind will help reduce phone time and are also effective with drop-in visitors.

SET LIMITS FOR CALLS

Establish a contract when you call by stating from the beginning that you only have a certain number of minutes. Also make calls just before lunch or at the end of the day, times when people are more likely to expedite a conversation.

CHANGE YOUR FURNITURE ARRANGEMENT

A bank manager once contacted my firm for help coping with

interruptions. As I studied his office, the reason he was struggling became clear. His office, glassed in on three sides, practically asked for interruptions. His desk faced the glass, and anyone passing by was within three feet of him. As people walked by, he would look up and nod. They would wave and often stick their heads in the door to make a brief comment. No wonder he was distracted. The solution, turning his desk around, was simple. With his back to the glass, he couldn't see them, and they couldn't catch his attention without a major effort.

Examine your office arrangement with productivity in mind. Your immediate work area should not be too comfortable or accessible for guests. If possible, turn your desk away from open doorways. Relocate your phone so when you're using it, you face away from the door and are less likely to be interrupted. And make sure you have good desk lighting.

STAND UP

When an uninvited visitor drops in, stand up to greet them and remain standing. Offering a seat makes a visitor feel welcome, and once seated, they are difficult to unseat. If you stand and walk toward the door, they get the message that you'll see them, but only for a moment. Try to remain courteous as you subtly move unwanted visitors away.

SAY "YES" WHEN ASKED IF YOU'RE BUSY

People tend to say "no" when someone pops in and inquires if you're busy. Don't hesitate to say, "Yes." Another response is to say "Yes, I am now, but I won't be at four. Could you come back then?" Or say, "I can't talk now, but what if I come to your office when I finish?" This latter response gives you control of the visit, when it occurs and how long it lasts.

WALK YOUR VISITOR

If a visitor takes too long, and you're getting antsy, stand up and say, "Why don't I walk with you back to your office?" And walk to the door, open it and walk the visitor down the hall. This technique is friendly, while moving the other person away from your office.

AVOID CHITCHAT WITH DROP-IN VISITORS

As with telephone calls, never ask an unexpected visitor, "How are you?" unless you want to know. Ask them, "What's up?" or "How can I help you?" This language sends a signal that you are in a strictly business frame of mind.

HANG UP A SIGN

Posting a sign on your door or doorknob is a direct, yet light-hearted manner of telling others you are busy. Close your door and hang a *Do Not Disturb, Work on Board* or *Hard At Work* sign where visitors will see it. In a fun way, these slogans remind people of your tight deadline. Most of them will respect your need for privacy. And remember, privacy equals productivity.

SAY "NO" EFFECTIVELY

Most people go through life thinking that "no" is a four-letter word. Making too many commitments, you get out of balance, rushing here and there. The solution to this anxiety could be learning to say "no" without feeling guilty. Your refusals should be clear, but pleasant.

Give options to the other person such as "No, I'm sorry. I can't, but maybe Louis could." Or "I was talking to Sherry at lunch today, and she might be interested." This technique helps the other person move forward without obligating you.

Get rid of guilt when refusing a new commitment.

An easy out is to blame your schedule: "I'm sorry, but my schedule would not allow it at this time." Or, try "Thank you for asking, but right now I just don't have the time."

Many times, particularly with friends, people feel obligated to say "yes." If you agree to participate despite no real interest in the project, you may tend to procrastinate or overlook the request altogether. At this point, the friendship starts to deteriorate on both sides. You are frustrated with yourself for getting involved, and your friend is upset because the work was left undone. Saying "no" at the beginning would have been better. Let that sense of obligation be a warning to back off. It will save time, as well as relationships.

LEAVE PRECISE MESSAGES

When you can't reach someone, leave specific messages. If appropriate, tell them *why* you called so they can be prepared when they call back. Also tell them *when* to call, stating a time you'll be available. For instance, say, "You can reach me at my office between 3:30 and 5:00 this afternoon."

INSTALL A PRIVATE LINE

A private telephone line is helpful for screening calls. Install a second, private line and release the number sparingly. I have a line for which only key people in my life know the number. When that line rings, I know it's important.

USE "HOLD" TIME

You could get annoyed when put on hold, or you could get busy. Go through your ACTION file while you wait. Pick out small, nagging projects to do. In the few minutes you're on hold, you could add business cards to your telephone directory, write a thank you note, or sign off on invoices.

FAX FOR ATTENTION

Since people generally read faxes before their phone messages or ordinary mail, consider sending a fax the next time you have trouble getting through to someone by phone. Enlarge a standard phone message slip on the copier, fill in your name, number and message, and fax it with an URGENT! notation.

AVOID BEGINNING OF THE DAY CONVERSATIONS

Many office workers like to start their day with chitchat — pouring coffee and leisurely catching up on news. Avoid this temptation. Monday mornings are particularly troublesome as people like to discuss their weekend activities. Steer clear of the chatterboxes (no matter how interesting their stories), go straight to your desk, and save your remarks for later.

CALL YOURSELF

Call yourself to double-check your voice mail message. Make sure it is clear, complete and encourages callers to leave specific messages. If you know what a caller wants, you can be prepared with the right files or your calendar or whatever you need on hand. My message informs callers they have three minutes to leave a detailed, confidential message.

ON THE
ROAD AGAIN

Skyrocketing costs in the travel industry are forcing companies, large and small, to take a hard look at their travel budgets. Businesses are cutting back on travel and using technology like video conferencing to eliminate unnecessary trips. Even so, the number of business travelers increases yearly, with close to 40 million people toting briefcases around the world last year.

Few executives can avoid hitting the road as meetings, conferences, and conventions beckon them from the four corners of the earth. Whether it's across town or across country, travel takes time. Most executives rate travel up there with meetings as a flagrant time waster. But a little preparation and ingenuity can make travel more productive and less stressful.

According to a *Priority Management* report, the average American will spend five years waiting in line during his lifetime. For the traveling executive, it may be even longer, figuring the waits at terminals, baggage claim, ticket counters and rental car stations.

Even waiting in line need not deal a blow to your productivity. From the highway to the concourse, you can beat the waiting game if you're properly armed.

This chapter will show you some practical ways to reduce

or avoid waiting time and make your travels as productive and profitable as possible.

PART ONE

PREPARING FOR TAKEOFF

For the frequent traveler, nothing beats the Boy Scout motto: Be Prepared. The following tips on preparation will make trips easier and get you on the road faster. Many of them can be done one time and serve you for many trips to follow.

CARRY A READ FILE

Keep a READ file (see Chapter 3) in your car or briefcase at all times. Then you'll have it with you wherever you might have to wait — a doctor's office, subway station, bank, client appointment, or even a traffic jam. Many times, my READ file has come in handy when I've been held up waiting for an accident to clear on the Interstate. While everyone else flips radio channels, honks their horns and gets angry, I vent my frustration by catching up on my reading.

BAG IT

Gather some basic supplies like pens, cards, and stamped envelopes and put them in a small bag or pocket of your carry-on luggage. When you've got a short wait ahead, you can pull out the supplies and use the time to write personal notes. Since keeping in touch with people is part of my rear view mirror perspective, I can work toward this goal while I wait.

PREPACK

Determine the standard items you need for a business trip — from socks and personal items to handkerchiefs and nightwear — and keep them packed. I keep one travel suit including shoes and hosiery clean and ready to go in a suit bag. Other items to prepack might include a travel clock, ties, and a small umbrella. If you keep these items packed and use them only for travel, you can finish packing in minutes without forgetting anything. I can be out my door in seven minutes using this one technique.

BUY EXTRA SUPPLIES
Purchase an extra set of toiletry items and prepack them in your suitcase. I like to buy small trial-size bottles and collect the courtesy soaps and shampoos offered at some hotels. If I don't like the brands, I simply empty the bottles and refill with my own favorites.

USE A CHECKLIST
A checklist for packing will help you remember all those items that can't be easily prepacked. For instance, cab fare, plane tickets, passport and hair dryer might be on your checklist. I keep this list on a 3x5 card in my calendar, but it could also be kept in your luggage. At the hotel, use this list to pack for the trip home so that you leave nothing behind.

GO WITH GREENBACKS
Traveler's checks can be lifesavers when you are short of cash and have no time to go to the bank. Purchase a small quantity to keep on hand. You can prepack the booklet of checks in your luggage or put them in a safe, but accessible place. Combined with a plastic card, traveler's checks can take you anywhere you have to go. On the road, they'll save you time waiting to cash a personal check at a bank or your hotel. A friend of mine flew 28,000 miles one month and used only a credit card and small traveler's checks. Hassle-free travel!

MANAGE YOUR ABSENCE
Before leaving the office on an extended trip, manage your absence by preparing colleagues and subordinates to help out. Alert them as to possible problems or crises that might arise and coach them on resolving matters. Appoint someone to handle routine matters while you are gone. It's a good idea to

request a memo or note from your "assistants," detailing what transpired in your absence. By preparing others, you avoid returning to a desk stacked with paperwork and problems that will interfere with effective follow-up to the business conducted away from the office.

EXPAND YOUR ITINERARY

Have your secretary prepare an itinerary that lists more than the standard where and when. Include contact names *with* phone numbers, directions if needed, meeting locations, rental car company with phone and reservation numbers, hotels with phone and confirmation numbers, times and the purpose for each appointment. If you're running late or miss a flight, you won't have to dig through a pile of folders to figure out whom to call with an explanation. And if you need to add an appointment while on the road, you can see at a glance when you'll have time.

Try to keep this document with you at all times. You can add important information to it as you travel. For instance, you might jot down the color, make, model and license tag number of your rental car in case memory fails you.

PREPARE YOUR CAR

If driving your own car, consider buying a citizens-band radio, flashlight, and jumper cables for emergencies. Check your spare tire for proper air pressure, put some change for tolls in the glove compartment and make sure you have appropriate maps. An old towel is also useful for any number of purposes including wiping fog from the inside of the windshield, catching crumbs from snack foods and cushioning your lower back. Additionally, in winter I store an extra blanket and a flare just to be on the "safe" side.

RENT A FAX MAILBOX

When you're on the go, faxed documents can keep pace if you open a fax mailbox. A service offered by major telephone companies, this electronic storage system allows travelers at hotels, airports or wherever to retrieve faxes at their convenience. Just call a toll-free number to check for faxes and have them downloaded to a nearby machine. You can charge the service to your calling card. Check with your phone company for details regarding fees, procedures and extras such as beeper options and voice-mail messages.

FAX BY LAPTOP COMPUTER

Instead of packing, carrying or finding a fax machine, consider using a laptop computer while you're on the road. Not only can it streamline your paperwork, but it can also send text-only faxes with the push of a few buttons. Services provided by organizations such as phone companies or computer networks can receive and retransmit your faxes to one or more locations. Or, you can invest in some fax software and send documents directly to their destinations.

BACK UP COMPUTER FILES

Before traveling, make a copy on a floppy disk of your laptop's operating software and important files and pack it. That way, if something should go wrong with the system, you won't be toting a useless machine. Just reload and get back to work.

PART TWO

MAKING THE SKIES FRIENDLY WHEN FLYING

Flying is a way of life for many executives. The hours spent in airplanes and airports might be your best time to relax, take a nap or read a novel. Or, it might also be your most productive office environment.

The very things that make plane travel relaxing — no ringing telephones, no drop-in visitors, no overflowing in-boxes — make it an attractive work area. If you're willing to give up that snooze and put down that bestseller, you can be even more productive in the air than at the office. Though you can't improve airline food, you can ease some frustrations by following these suggestions for making the friendly skies friendlier.

USE A TRAVEL AGENT

Employ the expertise of a good travel agent. Calling airlines yourself to book flights can get complicated with all the different rates and advance booking windows. Travel agents can book hotel and car rental services, while finding you the right flight for the right price. They will also furnish extra copies of your itinerary, saving you time writing it down for family and office members.

Let your agent know your flying preferences. Our travel agent is worth her weight in gold. She always reserves aisle seats for me and orders special, low-fat meals. She can frequently give us recommendations on restaurants and entertainment and make the necessary reservations.

JOIN AN AIRLINE CLUB

Frequent travelers should consider joining one of the clubs maintained by most airlines in all major airports. I think they are worth the fee. Club personnel will check you in, cutting time in line at the airline's desk. The club's lounge provides desks or tables where you can work, as well as telephones, computers, copiers, and other office services.

Geared toward the business traveler, these clubs offer a quiet environment and few distractions from your work. More and more, I see good time managers using their airport down time to advantage — working on laptops, making phone calls and faxing from these lounges.

FLY FIRST CLASS

If corporate guidelines allow, consider flying first class. The quieter atmosphere, roomier seats and efficient service contribute to a better work environment than other passenger classes.

Depending on how much you accomplish, the class upgrade may pay for itself through your increased productivity. First-class passengers can also board and deplane early without waiting in lines.

TAKE DIRECT FLIGHTS
Cutting down on changes and layovers will significantly reduce your flying time. Direct flights are usually worth the odd hours and price differences when you consider the hassle and time involved in changing planes. Having logged over 100,000 miles by air last year, I can vouch for the time-saving value of direct flights.

AVOID HUBS
If you must change planes, try to make connections in smaller cities and avoid "hub" airports, a regional home base through which most of an airline's flights are routed. Hub airports like Chicago's O'Hare almost guarantee delayed flights and missed connections. They are often congested and confusing. And when bad weather rolls in, it is harder to get flights out.

AVOID SKYWAY RUSH HOURS
If possible, stay out of the skies during the Christmas and Thanksgiving holidays. Crowded airports and crowded airplanes mean longer lines and longer delays, as well as problems with overbooked flights.

Airports are generally busiest between 4 p.m. and 7 p.m., so try to fly at other times. Depending on my schedule, I try to get flights out about 3:30 or 7:30, and many times will get home more quickly this way.

TAILOR YOUR WORK TO THE FLIGHT
Bring work suited to the length of the flight. Short flights are great for dictating letters, writing memos or tackling other short projects. Longer flights give you time for bigger projects such as preparing a speech, analyzing reports, or reading lengthy material. Don't forget to bring a calculator, laptop computer, notepad, dictaphone or other items needed to complete your projects. This book was largely written in the air

as I decided the chapters could be easily outlined or written on a plane.

CARRY HAND LUGGAGE

When possible, carry your bags onto the plane to avoid waiting in baggage claim. Rather than packing in one large suitcase that would have to be checked, try two bags, one stored in the overhead compartment and one under your seat. Some luggage manufacturers are marketing bags, specifically designed for the business traveler, featuring expandable pockets and divisions for files and paperwork. Remember when traveling, less is best, so pack lightly.

AVOID THE LAST FLIGHT

Whether a flight cancellation, engine trouble, or your own mistake causes you to miss a flight, if it's the last one of the day, you'll have no alternatives. In cities with more than one airport, such as Los Angeles or New York, you may be able to take a cab to another location. More likely, you will be stranded. Try to avoid this situation by scheduling earlier flights.

CATCH A RIDE

Arranging a ride to and from the airport can save you an hour or more at some airports. Many times, by the time you find a parking space and walk or take a shuttle to the airline counter, you have lost quite a bit of time. It's much simpler and faster to take a cab or have someone drop you at the curb outside your airline's ticket counter.

DEPLANE LATE

When arriving their destinations, coach class passengers should continue working until others have deplaned. You'll save time and aggravation by letting the aisle crowd thin out. First-class passengers can easily deplane ahead of the crowd or wait until later. It's amazing to me how many people jump up, grab their bags and stand in the aisle for 10 to 15 minutes, for the plane doors to open. In that amount of time, each one could have read an article, responded to letters or reviewed a report.

CARRY ON CRITICAL ITEMS

You never know when an airline might lose your luggage. It can happen to you, so keep key materials with you. Critical documents or supplies for your business appointments as well as prescriptions, eyeglasses and other important personal items should be hand carried onto the plane.

BYPASS THE TICKET COUNTER CROWD

If you miss a connecting flight and there are lines at the ticket counter, find a phone. Call the airline's reservation number or your travel agent and reserve a seat. Then go to the ticket counter to pick up your ticket. That way, the flight won't get fully booked while you're waiting in line. And you won't have to scramble all over the airport looking for another flight.

CARRY A POCKET FLIGHT GUIDE

If you find yourself changing flight schedules during trips, carry a pocket-sized Official Airline Guide (OAG). This directory provides information on all U.S. flights, including flight times, numbers, stops, and reservation telephone numbers.

If your airline changes or cancels your flight, this booklet saves you time and dollars. A quick look at the guide tells you where you can go, when the flight leaves and whom to call. If your company subscribes to the full-sized version, photocopy the pages covering your destinations and home city and take the copies with you for reference.

AVOID RENTING CARS

Some cities practically demand car rentals, but many do not. Rental cars can be big time wasters, so use them only when necessary. Checking them in and out, filling up with gas, parking, and driving in an unfamiliar town consumes valuable time. And renting a car may be more expensive than hopping a cab to your appointments.

CLAIM RENTAL CARS BEFORE BAGGAGE
If you must rent a car, process the paperwork before claiming your baggage. Rather than heading to baggage claim with the crowd from your flight, go take care of the car first. By the time you're done, your bags should be waiting.

JOIN CAR CLUBS
Taking advantage of the special services offered by some car rental services can save hours. We belong to an agency that offers Gold service, which means we have no paperwork to process. At one agency, company CEOs can join its Platinum Club in which cars are delivered to you at the airport.

HOLD CONVENIENT MEETINGS
When you're in charge, consider holding meetings or seminars at the airport or airport hotels. Many airports have quiet facilities for business meetings, and the hotels have conference rooms for rent. You'll save the time and trouble of traveling to an off-site location and perhaps catch an earlier flight home.

CHECK OUT YOUR DRIVERS
When booking limousine service, have your travel agent or secretary specifically request a driver that speaks English and who is familiar with the city.

FORWARD YOUR ITINERARY
Forward a copy of your itinerary to the limousine service. Drivers can then plan your transportation routes and avoid mistakes. Even when the driver has your schedule, don't hesitate to confirm your destination and times with him. On a trip to Phoenix, a driver took me to the wrong hotel. My host company was in charge of providing the limousine service my itinerary. When the driver picked me up at the airport, I failed to double check his destination. I ended up at a hotel on the

opposite side of town from where I needed to be, costing me two hours of valuable time.

PART THREE
CHOOSING A HOTEL

Business travel is big business. Business travelers spent an estimated $66 million to $100 million in 1990 and are projected to spend more each year. Innkeepers, eager for a slice of the pie, are taking giant steps to court the corporate market. Never before have hotels been so accommodating for the executive on the road.

GET DOWN TO BUSINESS
Select a hotel that caters to business travelers. Some hotels have fully-equipped business centers that give you access to computers, fax machines and copiers. At other places, a concierge will obtain typing and fax services for you by calling a list of independent contractors. If you carry your own equipment — portable computer, printer, or fax machine — request a room with modified outlets for handling the machines' energy requirements. Whatever your needs, make sure the hotel can meet them before you register.

REQUEST THE CONCIERGE LEVEL
Many hotels now offer concierge levels for the business traveler. For a fee, you stay in designated rooms, convenient to an area where the hotel provides a variety of services. Meals, newspapers, telephones and sometimes business equipment are available. A concierge will be there to assist you with flights, directions, shuttle reservations and other tasks.

I use the concierge level primarily in the morning. I can get a quick, no-fuss breakfast from the buffet without waiting in the hotel restaurant. The selection is great for a traveler's diet — fresh fruits, pastries, cereals and high-fiber, low-fat items. And I can network with other business people, scan a newspaper and make free local phone calls in a comfortable, informal setting.

USE EXPRESS CHECKOUT

We have found many people are afraid of express checkout because they don't know how to use it. The hotel usually provides directions, but if you're still confused after reading them, don't hesitate to call the front desk. Someone should be able to give you a detailed explanation. Once you get the hang of it, and it's really very simple, you'll never want to face those checkout lines again.

Many hotels also have video checkout, allowing you to view your bill on the television screen. After checking the charges, just drop off your key or leave it in your room.

Leaving a hotel in New York recently, I passed by more than a hundred people in the checkout line. They were there to cash checks, check out and obtain information. If they had used express checkout and brought traveler's checks, most of those people would never have had to wait.

GUARANTEE YOUR HOTEL RESERVATIONS

Ask your travel agent or secretary to guarantee your hotel reservations with a charge card. No matter how late your arrival, the hotel must reserve your room.

Have the hotel phone number and the reservation confirmation number added to your detailed itinerary. If there is any question about your reservation, you'll have the guarantee number at your fingertips.

SOUND THE ALARM

Rather than rely solely on a telephone wake-up call, bring your own alarm clock on important trips. Wake-up calls are frequently late and sometimes overlooked. A travel alarm clock, which can be prepacked, gives you double assurance of making it up on time.

Even though many hotels now provide clock/radios with alarms, I still carry my own battery-operated travel alarm as a backup. This proved helpful on one trip when an ice storm caused a power failure from 1 to 3 a.m. The next morning, I was up on time and ready, while my companions were in a frenzy because they were late.

CHECK OUT THE SHUTTLE

Major hotels in large cities frequently subscribe to an airport limousine service. The shuttle usually follows a route among several hotels, picking up customers, then heading for the airport. Convenient and generally less expensive than a taxi, these shuttles have drawbacks. Before hopping on one, ask how many more stops between your hotel and the airport. If several stops remain, it may be worth the time and a few dollars to call a cab.

AN EYE FOR DETAIL

Although most of this book focuses on work productivity, these last two chapters look at your life away from the office. This chapter examines practical pointers for saving time at home. The next one takes a broader view, asking the question, "What can you do in your off-hours to build your enthusiasm and keep your perspective from day to day and week to week?"

According to a *Priority Management* report, the average American will spend a total of six months waiting at stoplights, four years doing housework, and six years eating. Obviously, activities away from the office could stand a little streamlining!

A big trash can, good scheduling, and people skills are keys for managing your home efficiently.

As with managing your professional life, the work of ordering your home life has a few requirements: liberal use of a trash can, accurate scheduling, and sharpening your people skills.

No doubt you have developed many of your own techniques for saving time while housekeeping, cooking, shopping and caring for the kids. Here are a few of my favorites.

PART ONE

FINANCES

In this day of downsizing, protecting our finances is vital. Yet as I travel, I find few people take the time to outline their financial plan. Recently when working with a group of professionals whose average annual income is $185,000, everybody told me their finances were out of order and how in debt they were. It's important to be financially solvent and creating a binder is a giant leap toward seeing the big picture of your finances.

CREATE A PERSONAL FINANCE BINDER

You don't have to be an accountant to keep your dollars and cents straight. Purchase either a financial file or a three-ring binder with pocket dividers and paper. In this binder, collate your financial records and keep them up to date. Having this information at your fingertips is helpful when you are making any kind of financial decision. You can tell at a glance where your assets and liabilities lie and where there's room for improvement.

Many people know the state of the economy better than their family finances.

Make sure someone close to you knows where this file is located — it could be a vital resource should you become incapacitated. It takes little time to assemble and can save you and your family much time and anxiety in the long run.

Topics to cover in your quick access financial file include:

- *Bills.* Every time you pay bills, file them or note them in this binder.
- *Stocks and Bonds.* List them and track their value on a regular basis.
- *Bank Accounts.* List the locations and account numbers

for your checking, savings, and other deposit accounts.

- *Safe Deposit Box.* Record the contents, its location and number, and the location of the key.

- *Retirement Fund.* Where are your retirement accounts, what kind are they, and how much are they worth?

- *Assets and Liabilities.* Itemize your assets and liabilities so you know at all times what you are worth.

- *Emergency Information.* Catalog important information for your family in case of emergency. Include everyone's blood type, allergies to medications, and any special health conditions.

- *Insurance.* For each type of insurance you carry (life, medical, car, disability, and homeowners, for instance), record the name of your carrier, the policy number, the location of the policy and a contact person at the carrier company.

- *Automobile.* For each car, list the type, insurance information, maintenance records, and loan status.

- *Real Estate.* List all your property with insurance, mortgage and tenant information.

- *Emergency Numbers.* List your attorneys, bankers, minister, relatives and neighbors to call in an emergency.

- *Charge Accounts.* List the accounts and their numbers. If you have it, record a central number for canceling all your charge accounts. A friend of mine photocopies her credit cards and carries one copy in her suitcase and keeps one in this file.

- *Other.* Make a note of any other business interests.

HAVE CHECKS DIRECT-DEPOSITED
Direct deposit of your paychecks and other regular payments will save you a trip to the bank. Many people also prefer to have automatic deductions from their bank accounts for utilities and other bills.

SYSTEMATIZE YOUR BILL PAYING

Too often paying bills is a random process — when a few pile up, you pay them. For a couple of months, keep a record of when your bills arrive. Look over the log and determine one or two days a month you could pay bills and still meet your deadlines and obligations. For many people, these dates fall around the first and middle of the month. Then mark throughout your calendar the days you will pay bills and stick to these dates.

As bills arrive, keep them together in a pre-designated location so you won't have to search several places to find them all. And keep everything you need for paying them — stamps, pens, and envelopes, for instance — nearby.

A few years ago, I had a file folder labeled BILLS that I kept in the top drawer of my front hall table. As I sorted the mail on this table each day, the bills went directly into this file. Now I use four magnetic, acrylic folders, placed on the side of the refrigerator — one for bills and one for each of our three family members.

PART TWO

PAPERWORK

CLEAN OUT YOUR FILES

Who needs 30-year-old bank statements and outdated warranties? Spend an afternoon weeding your storage files and boxes. Toss out any paperwork that has expired or lost its value to you.

AVOID THE POST OFFICE

The post office is one place I can always count on standing in line. There are many ways to sidestep these lines:

- Buy stamps by mail. Obtain some forms from the post office. You can fill out a request, mail it in with a check and receive your stamps by mail at no extra cost.

- Find other distributors. Stamps are available at other locations. Look for the postal emblem at grocery stores and news stands and buy stamps when you're making other purchases.

- Use mailing services. Some businesses specialize in providing mail services, are often more efficient and give you more options for mailing letters and packages.

- Go at off-hours. Lines are more likely to be shorter in mid-morning or mid-afternoon. The end of a business day is particularly crowded so if you must go at all, try to plan ahead and get to the post office earlier.

BUY BIRTHDAY CARDS EN MASSE

Buying cards ahead of time will save you any number of trips to the card shop. At the beginning of the year, make a list of all the cards you will need and buy them at one time.

You could buy a large quantity of a favorite, somewhat generic birthday card. Or, as I like to do, take a list of your friends and relatives to the store and buy them each a card. During the Super Bowl, I address and stamp all the envelopes and later sort the cards by month into my tickler file. When the time arrives, I jot down a note and mail it.

POST EMERGENCY NUMBERS

If your child has just swallowed rubbing alcohol, you don't want to consult the phone book to find the number for your local Poison Control Center. Post this important number, along with other emergency numbers near at least one phone on each floor of your house. Also post telephone numbers for doctors, relatives and neighbors you may need to reach during an emergency.

TOSS JUNK MAIL

Don't even look at your mail until you are near a wastebasket. Toss junk mail directly into the trash. Many times, I don't even open it. You can also discard envelopes and extraneous material, before sorting the rest into an action pile or bill compartment.

USE ADDRESS LABELS

Writing out your name and address takes approximately 45 seconds. With just a quick flick, address labels will save you time at home and at the office. My labels are done by computer in lots of 200.

ALPHABETIZE WARRANTIES AND INSTRUCTIONS

An easy way to organize warranties and mechanical instructions, which often take too much room in your file drawer, is to file them in an accordion file. Extra small parts, like the gadget for wall-mounting your telephone, can be stored with their related warranty. You could also use a three-ring binder, with clear, plastic sheets for holding odd-sized pieces of paper.

PART THREE

HOUSEHOLD

MAKE TV TIME PRODUCTIVE

I realize there are times when we just want to do nothing at all, and that's understandable. But research has shown that the average American spends more than four hours a day watching television. Think what you could gain by using this time productively.

If the television has you trapped, plan some things to do during that time in addition to watching your favorite sitcom. Update your photo albums. Organize a drawer from your desk or kitchen. Prepare the week's menu or grocery list. Write brief letters. Catch up on ironing. There are an endless number of small tasks you can accomplish while watching televison. Learn to make this time productive.

STOP SEARCHING FOR KEYS
How much time have you lost rummaging through drawers for your keys or searching the pockets of what you wore yesterday when they're really on the kitchen counter? Losing keys is an epidemic problem, but easily cured.

In my home, we installed a key holder beside the back door. When we come in, we hook them right there. You may prefer a bowl or drawer, but designate a particular spot for keys and use it.

MAKE KEY DUPLICATES
Get copies made of all your keys and write down where they are. Hide an extra house key somewhere outside your home, perhaps in a small box buried under a certain rock. Carry a duplicate car key in your wallet or give one to a family member or neighbor who could help you in an emergency.

MAINTAIN A SEWING KIT
Buy a sewing kit and keep it stocked. A few years ago, I requested a specific kit for Christmas. It is a simple, plastic box with a lid. Whatever container you select, keep all your sewing supplies together to avoid searching the house for those extra buttons that came with your blue shirt or that certain shade of green thread.

ORGANIZE YOUR SUPPLIES
Use small boxes or bins inside your drawers to organize stored items. In your desk, for example, you could devote a bin to "creative" supplies — glue, scissors, sparkles, stickers, colored markers, rubber cement, tape and other similar items. Then when you need to help a child with his art or science project, you can grab the box and have most necessities on hand. It sure saves the aggravation of searching cabinets and drawers

throughout the house for the Elmer's® Glue-all. And it saves 9:00 p.m. trips to the drug store in search of poster board.

GET PRESCRIPTIONS BY PHONE
Ask your doctor to phone in prescriptions to your local pharmacy, so they'll be ready when you arrive to pick them up.

REFUSE TELEPHONE SOLICITATION
Don't spend your valuable evening hours listening to telemarketers. No matter how worthy their cause, ask them to contact you by mail and politely hang up. I say, "I'm sorry. I do not take telephone solicitation." That ends the call nicely.

CLEAR YOUR KITCHEN COUNTER
It's easier to cook and clean when your kitchen counters are uncluttered. And fewer items will get dirty if they are stored elsewhere. If you only use that old mixer once a month, stow it underneath in a cabinet where it won't collect dust or get in your way.

SEPARATE SILVERWARE
When loading the dishwasher, separate your silverware as you go. Assign a different compartment in the basket to each type of utensil: forks, salad forks, soup spoons, serving spoons, knives and the like. If they're already sorted, unloading is easier and takes less time.

RETURN CALLS WHILE YOU'RE COOKING
Make sure your kitchen telephone is cordless or has an extended cord that will allow you freedom of movement. You can accomplish lots of kitchen duties from washing dishes to mixing while you're returning personal calls.

USE A CROCKPOT
How many people receive crockpots as wedding gifts, store them in the back corner cupboard, and never think of them

again? These devices can be great time-savers. Prepare the ingredients for a pot roast one night, place them in your crockpot the next morning, let it cook all day and a nutritious dinner will be waiting when you get home that night. Or set the timer to come on during the night and have hot oatmeal waiting for your family the next morning.

This is a great gadget that is often overlooked. There are wonderful, heart-wise recipes for it, too. It's a gift to yourself when you come home too tired to think about cooking, and a healthy meal is ready.

DOUBLE THE PORTIONS, HALVE THE TROUBLE

When preparing a meal, cook twice as much as you need. The extra portion can be frozen before or after cooking for a nice, quick meal at a later date. Remember to label what you freeze, so you don't waste time trying to discern what's under the foil wrap.

I double every possible recipe. One week a month, I reward myself by not cooking at all — we just thaw and heat meals that were prepared during the previous three weeks.

ORGANIZE YOUR GROCERY SHOPPING

Arrange your grocery list according to the layout of the store. Make a master list with a column for each department in the store, in the order you shop. My list has columns across the top of the page headed *Produce, Meats, Canned Goods, Snacks, Staples, Frozen Foods, Dairy, Breads, Soft Drinks,* and *Miscellaneous.* If you really want to be detailed, you can write in staples like flour and sugar on your master list. Then make copies of this document and post a fresh one on the refrigerator each week.

**Make a master list for grocery shopping
and try to shop only once a week.**

Whoever uses the last or nearly the last of any item must add it to the list in the proper category. If someone forgets, then it goes on next week's list. Only buy what is on the list and go to the store once a week, preferably at a scheduled time, unless an unexpected occasion arises. I like to go on Sunday afternoons. Before leaving for the store, think through your week's menus and add needed items. If you use this system, the list will be ready no matter who does the shopping or when.

ARRANGE YOUR CLOSET

Arrange the clothes in your closet by category, keeping suits, skirts, shirts, blouses, blazers and other items in separate sections. Instead of searching the entire closet for your ecru dress shirt, then finding it in the dry cleaning pile, you can go directly to the right section to see whether it's there. The same principle applies to jewelry. You can accessorize faster when earrings, necklaces, bracelets and other trinkets are organized.

I use three tie racks to organize accessories: one for belts, one for scarves and one for necklaces.

DOUBLE YOUR CLEANING SUPPLIES

If you live in a two-story house, buy an extra set of cleaning supplies, one set for upstairs and another for downstairs. Keep them in baskets with handles so the cleaners and brushes are easily transported from room to room.

PRE-SORT YOUR LAUNDRY

Buy three laundry baskets and label them *white, dark,* and *colors.* Place them in a convenient, central location and request family members to sort their dirty clothes into the right basket. Even very young children can master this task, and it will make life easier for whoever does the laundry. You can also tell quickly when you've got a full load waiting to be washed.

SORT LINENS BY BEDROOM

Organize your linen closet by bedroom, designating a shelf or part of a shelf for each room. If, as in our house, you have different sizes of beds, you'll save time trying to figure out if a particular sheet fits the double, queen-, or king-size bed.

I also like to strip a bed, wash the linens and put them right back on so I rarely have to fold them. If you can't stand the sight of a bare mattress, just throw on the comforter or bedspread until the sheets are ready.

PART FOUR

CHILDREN

One gift we can give our children, and it should be given at an early age, is independence. Encourage your children to be independent and earn yourself some time to boot.

ASSIGN KITCHEN DUTIES
Teach your children at an early age to help with kitchen duties. Not only do you save time, but it also gives them a sense of accomplishment and gives you an opportunity to praise them. Even a three- to four-year-old child can lighten your load by putting out place mats and napkins, taking silverware to the table, bringing dishes to the sink and stirring. Older children can set the table, take out trash, and bake simple recipes or mixes.

MONITOR BEDTIME STORIES
Few things can be as relaxing as reading a bedtime story with your child. But for those nights when you're feeling particularly tired or pressed for time, have some short books that can be discreetly selected from the stack. It also helps to start at an early age setting limits on the *number* of stories to be read. Children are experts at delaying bedtime and will "read" tirelessly if given the chance.

STOCKPILE SCHOOL SUPPLIES
Invest up front in your sanity by stockpiling school supplies. Go to your local discount store and purchase a large variety of

items from creative supplies like poster board to five-subject notebooks. You'll be prepared when little Mary surprises you with a craft project due the next day or loses her History notebook.

START YOUR GOOD MORNINGS THE NIGHT BEFORE

If you plan ahead for the next morning, your day will get off to a better start. Laying out your children's clothes and packing their lunches the night before school helps avoid confusion and a mad rush the next morning. In my family, we even pre-set our table for breakfast.

How you start the day often determines how the day will go.

These routines save precious time in the mornings, and how we start our day often determines how the day will go. If you arise to find a button missing on your jacket, shoes that need polishing and a stain on your tie, you can easily lapse into a bad mood. These delays make you leave home feeling rushed, anxious, and stressed. Your mood affects others, and everybody starts on a low note. If you prepare your clothes, housework and whatever needs to be done the next day, you head for the office with a smile, not a grimace. And you start the day a step ahead.

PUT YOUR HOME ON A CHILD'S SCALE

Children can do simple tasks for themselves if you place the resources within their reach. When you begin child-proofing to make a home safe for your toddler, think about child-scaling it, too. For instance, place toys, puzzles and books on lower shelves and cabinets so you won't have to hand them out. Make your little ones' spoons, bibs, and plastic dishes accessible so they can set their own places at the table. A five year old can pour his own juice if he can reach the pitcher and cups.

PART FIVE

SHOPPING

AVOID HOLIDAY SHOPPING

Waiting in line for gifts to be purchased and wrapped during the hectic holiday season eats up time. Shop early for the December holidays in particular, but reserve a little last minute shopping to help you get in the spirit of the season. Since many stores offer January sales, the first weeks of the year are great times to purchase Father's Day, Mother's Day and Valentine gifts.

SHOP BY PHONE

Shopping early may be impossible for some people. Another alternative is to shop by telephone. Many stores will accept phone orders, and catalogs are great time savers. If you want to personally wrap your gifts, have them shipped to you. Otherwise, direct delivery will save you time wrapping and mailing packages. Be sure to keep a record of what you ordered, the company, how much it cost and where it will be delivered.

SEND GIFT CERTIFICATES

When your ideas and time are dwindling, consider sending gift certificates. These make particularly good presents for people you don't know well such as a doctor or business associate, but whom you need to remember. Most restaurants, department stores, gift shops and mail-order companies offer gift certificates, which can often be purchased by mail or phone.

MAKE A DONATION

Another gift option is sending donations to charitable organizations. For Christmas one year, I received a card saying a donation in my name had been given to our local Crisis Control Center. Another Christmas, a group of us decided to donate toys to needy children in place of buying gifts for each other. Next year, I am going to duplicate this idea, choosing my own favorite charities. It's a win-win situation: you save time, a worthy organization gains resources, and the gift is meaningful.

HIRE A PERSONAL SHOPPER
Check with your local department stores to see if they offer personal shopping services. For clothing needs, you can give shoppers your sizes, style and color preferences and let them pull together some outfits for you, including accessories. And when something new comes in that they think suits you, many personal shoppers will give you a call. For gifts, tell them about the recipient, the occasion, and your price range, and they can suggest a selection of items to purchase.

THE PERSONAL CHALLENGE

I recently spoke to a large group of people in their forties and fifties. Each person completed a survey. As I studied the results, a common thread emerged. They wanted to know: "Is this all there is?" They had reached a point in their life spans that held no excitement for them. The present and the future, the state of their lives, was disappointing and bleak.

Here are a few of the comments made by these middle-aged executives:

- "I would like to run away and start over."
- "I never thought life would be this boring or mundane."
- "I could use some adventure in my life."
- "I'm not sure the energy I've put into my work has been worth it. I have lost my wife, kids, and most of my friends."

Could you be the author of these words? Like this group, large numbers of men and women have grown bored with their lives. They wish for different lifestyles with different people under different circumstances. These thoughts reflect the strain of demanding jobs that drain an executive's energy.

The job looms so large and becomes so absorbing that you have little time to recharge. At this point, life is out of balance. And you begin to question: "Is this all there is?" and "Is this my reward for 20 years of effort?"

Research shows that most executives are achievement oriented. As achievers, they tend to take on more and more activities and leadership responsibilities until the day, and sometimes the nights, are full. They come home late and leave home early just to stay above the swamp of paper and demands.

Executives wrapped up in their work easily forget about the long-term important issues. They forget to take care of significant relationships. In fact, these relationships become a hindrance, one more thing to do and one more person to see. Relationships outside the office become an imposition, although they could be your source of refreshment and inspiration. By being so busy achieving, you become isolated from those people who form the foundations of your life — spouse, father, mother, children, and others. Is this the price you're willing to pay for success on the job?

In the competition for your attention, work usually wins. People lose.

Women often tell me their executive husbands are boring, tired, uncreative, have routine sex lives and don't talk. They are *on* around others — friendly and open. As soon as business concludes, the *other self* appears — tired, burned out, stressed, and wanting to be left alone.

Women executives, too, are suffering. They work long hours, juggle many activities and are still the family nurturers. They secretly resent carrying the burden of emotional responsibilities as well as the hands-on activities of the family by themselves.

In both men and women, the crowded, tense circumstances of their lives have produced an undercurrent of anger that this life is not what they thought it would be.

Where did things go wrong? One reason is failing to look in the rear view mirror. Ultimately, this perspective or "retrospective" reminds you that there is more to life than your career. You see a number of images, including relationships you want to have when you're no longer active in the business arena. When you picture yourself at age 102, you realize you don't want to be alone, living a life of "I wish I had ..." or "Why didn't I ...?" In addition to setting professional goals, you understand the need to nurture other areas of life, particularly your relationships and health.

A look in the rear view mirror helps you realize the importance of relationships.

You can get so absorbed in business that you forget what is really going to make you happy in the long run. To avoid losing your close relationships and your good health, you must find a balance between career and personal goals.

Often the busy schedule of an executive makes these two activities extremely difficult. Travel schedules, meetings, deadlines, and projects line up to steal your time, plus some. At the end of a long day, it's difficult to eat well, do something physical, and invest in relationships. Instead, you have a drink, smoke a cigarette, watch television and "chill out." Significant others get pushed to the background. One day leads to another, and a routine is established. Soon this routine blocks out the very people that are most important in our lives and demolishes exercise and nutrition.

It's an easy pattern to fall into. I fight it, too. After logging 130,000 flyer miles in less than six months last year, I had to take a harsh look at my life. Every night I was falling into bed in another hotel and dreading the next day. I had gained weight and lost touch with my family. I had to ask myself, "Is this the lifestyle I want?" I had to peek once more in the rear view mirror and change my ways.

After reframing my vision, I decided more of my goals would have a personal focus. Now, each day, I try to do something for myself — eating a fat-free diet, exercising 30 minutes, or doing something nice for my family.

I believe you can maintain this personal focus and at the same time achieve professional success. In fact, taking time out, renewing your personal life and health, helps prevent burnout. By giving you a fresh perspective and enthusiasm, finding this balance enhances your success. You will work more efficiently and effectively on the job and enjoy your life more as a whole.

That is the personal challenge: to become successful without losing the real priorities. Next time you're out to dinner, look around the restaurant. How many couples do you see, eating in silence? No conversation, just another dinner. They have no fun, no interaction. They're bored. They are probably asking themselves, "Is this all there is?" Unless they can reframe the relationship, "yes" is the answer to this question.

The solution is managing your life so that you have time for fun, creativity, and a healthy lifestyle. This chapter addresses the challenge of finding a balance.

TAKE TIME OUT

When you are working and have a zillion things to do, it is easy to just keep going, working longer hours and more days. But what you really need is a Time Out. Take some time to recharge your batteries. Getting away from work, if only for an hour, can yield a different, fresher perspective.

I recharge by walking and listening to music. These activities give me time to look at the world from a serene plane. Feeling reinvigorated, I am then ready to tackle the challenges of work.

Like short Time Outs, vacations can be good medicine for your work and your marriage. A friend of mine, a free-lance writer, takes regular, extended Time Outs. Her last one was a trip to Ecuador, one she said she could ill afford. But she reported great results — new ideas and enthusiasm for her writing.

PRACTICE POSITIVE SELF TALK

Positive reinforcement is a boost to our success. Though you may think it must come from others, positive self talk can also come from within. The more your brain hears of your success, the more successful you will be, no matter who the speaker is.

PLAN TIME FOR FAMILY

Furthering relationships with others, particularly your significant other, requires time. Plan to spend special times with the ones you love. My husband and I regularly schedule two- or three-day trips to spend time as a couple. We leave all our work behind. We talk. We laugh. And we ultimately strengthen our relationship during these times.

Your children also need some of your prime time. My son used to tell me, "Mom, you're not listening. I want you to listen with your eyes." We need to tune to our children's channel, look them in the eye and give them our full attention.

SCHEDULE ONE EXCITING ACTIVITY EVERY DAY

Planning exciting activities will keep you from getting into routines with nothing to brighten your days. Look at your calendar for the week and schedule a tennis match one day, an hour to listen to music, a trip to the park with your children or some other activities you would enjoy. I like to schedule 30 minutes to read part of a novel or plan dinner with friends at a new restaurant.

If you never *plan* for excitement, you may find it in destructive, rather than productive, avenues. A car passed me on the Interstate recently, doing at least 85 miles per hour. A few minutes later, I saw the driver stopped by a highway patrol officer. Soon, he passed me again, gunning his motor down city streets. I wonder if this man lacks excitement in his life, and driving recklessly gives him a thrill. Or perhaps he finds excitement by over-scheduling, making his adrenaline flow as he speeds between appointments. Whatever the reason, it is far better to plan your exciting activities than to take excessive chances in everyday situations.

PUT WORRY IN PERSPECTIVE

Successful people put their worries in the right time frame. They make the best decision they can — right or wrong — with the information available, and then they move on. A lot of other people refuse to rebound. They drag worries around like a heavy sack slung over their shoulders. And they drag others down with them.

People in any sphere of life, personal or business, who have the ability to bounce back from bad situations stand out from the pack. Successful people are positive and fun. They have their share of crises, but they move forward instead of wasting time looking back at their failures. Other people are worriers and gee-zers: "Oh, gee, why didn't I ...?" Worry drains your energy. Put it in its proper perspective and use your energy in productive ways.

GEAR YOURSELF TO BE EARLY

Avoid the stress of being chronically late. When you plan too tightly or delay unnecessarily, you encourage stress by making yourself late. Try to be early for appointments. If you must wait, do something productive like reading articles in your READ file or writing quick notes.

I have a friend who calls to say she is coming to town and will arrive at three in the afternoon. Nobody, however, puts 3 p.m. on his calendar, because we know she will be at least an hour late. Being late gets any appointment off to a bad start, is poor business, and is stress-inducing.

HAVE AN ACTIVE SOCIAL LIFE

Cultivating friends and activities unrelated to your business interests gives your life an exciting dimension. You can also enjoy these people and events with your spouse, who won't feel like an outsider or mere adjunct to your career.

You could start by supporting the arts in your community. Attending a play or an art showing is a great way to escape the pressures of your work and get problems out of your mind if only for a few hours. Like a good night's sleep, such a break can renew your mental energy and supply you with fresh ideas.

HAVE BREAKFAST WITH FRIENDS
Few things are as rewarding as spending quality time with friends. But with the commitments of work and family, friendships often falter. One way to stay in touch is to schedule breakfast dates. Knowing you have to be at the office by a certain hour, you have a built-in time limit that your friend can understand. In just an hour over breakfast, you can cover lots of ground and start your day on a positive note.

RELAX
Can you relax in your home? If the house is too messy to relax, hire a cleaning service. If you have meetings four nights out of every five, learn to say "no" more effectively. If cooking, eating, cleaning the kitchen and getting the kids to bed takes four hours every evening, buy some frozen dinners or find some microwave recipes or make dinner a team effort. Busy people tend to view their time at home as expendable and fill it with tasks. Everyone needs a little time each night to recharge their batteries. Make sure you can relax at home.

TURN OFF THE TELEVISION
Try living six weeks without the television. Too often, TV becomes a substitute for relationships. In many homes, it's a companion for adults and a baby-sitter for children. How often do you schedule your family around your favorite shows? "Wait until *Cheers* is over, sweetheart, and I'll help you with your homework." If you'll turn off the television and concentrate on building your family ties, you'll reap the rewards in the long run.

In my family, we got rid of television for six months. The first week was stressful. But after the initial withdrawal phase, we hardly missed it. The time away from the television allowed us to get reacquainted as a family. We talked, played games, and even the children began to enjoy reading.

FORESTALL THE TRAVEL BLUES

A job that takes you on the road frequently can leave your loved ones feeling blue. Take a few precautions to ease the pain of separation, particularly with children who may have trouble understanding why you're leaving:

- Call daily to report your progress and, more importantly, listen to their activities and concerns.

- Discuss your work and what you'll be doing on the trip.

- Resolve family problems and finish household projects before departure.

- Schedule a special activity that everyone will look forward to doing when you return, even if it's just an evening with a favorite video and popcorn.

RETURN BORROWED ITEMS

How many times do you look at a garden tool or book and remind yourself to return it? Then you forget about it for another two weeks. Go through your house and collect everything you've borrowed. Then return one item every day until the pile is gone. It'll relieve your guilt and improve your relationships.

WRITE IT DOWN

Don't rely on your memory. A calendar can be a lifeline to worry-free living. Make notes in it to remember even small tasks like returning a library book or calling about your property taxes or making notes from a telephone call. You'll free your mind to enjoy the people and events in your life.

COMMIT TO LEISURE TIME

Leisure time is as good for you as vitamins or exercise. Plan for unoccupied time in your schedule. By giving to yourself, you have more to share and give to others in your office and your life.

SURPRISE OTHERS
When clients complain to me of their dull lives, the first question that comes to mind is: "When is the last time YOU did something to make your relationships work?" Think back to the last time you did something really nice for the significant people in your life. Simple surprises can have a powerful impact. A phone call, a card, a bouquet of wildflowers are inexpensive ways to invest in a relationship.

RELAX YOUR STANDARDS
Life will go on even if you don't get the tomatoes planted this week or even this season. It may be more important to spend those Saturdays at your child's Little League games than in your garden. Think of your priorities and don't be afraid to let unimportant tasks slide.

COUNT YOUR BLESSINGS
When stress or problems threaten to bog you down, start counting your blessings. Taking a positive outlook can carry you over the waves and land you at home in good humor.

UNPLUG THE PHONE
If it's the only way to unwind at home, unplug the telephone. Just don't forget to reconnect it later. You could also set the answering machine to pick up calls before the telephone rings.

GET ENOUGH SLEEP
Some people like Margaret Thatcher need only a few hours of sleep at night. Others need eight or more hours in order to function well the next day. Know your body clock and commit to getting the sleep you need. An occasional lapse is fine, but long-term shortages will leave you tired, grumpy, short-tempered and ineffective in making decisions. And the people most likely to bear the brunt of your ill humor will be the ones at home. If necessary, use an alarm clock to remind you to go to bed.

CHANGE THE PACE ON WEEKENDS

Arrange your time off to give you a change of pace from the office. If you spend most of your work time traveling and meeting with people, try to spend quiet weekends at home. If you have a number-crunching job at a desk 90 percent of the day, plan an active weekend with a trip to the mountains or some athletic pursuits. If you spend most of your week managing and relating to people, spend a Saturday refinishing a piece of furniture or doing some other task with defined limits and offering a sense of accomplishment.

KEEP A JOURNAL

Consider buying a notebook and writing in it regularly like a journal. Putting words on paper helps you clarify thoughts and feelings. And writing down your worries and problems can put them in perspective and lead you to logical solutions.

FORGIVE

Adopt a forgiving view of life and people. Carrying a grudge or grinding an axe not only wears you down, but also burdens the people close to you. Forgiving others frees you to focus on the parts of life you enjoy and appreciate.

LAUGH

Everyone needs a good laugh now and then. Not only does it relieve tension, but research now points to extensive physiological benefits of a hearty laugh. Many times business people are so absorbed in crises and responsibilities that opportunities for laughter pass by unnoticed. Try to take a lighter view of your circumstances and cultivate your sense of humor.

■　■　■　■　■

A Chinese proverb says the trip of a thousand miles begins with a single step. You can start today incorporating these time-saving tips. But the real question to address is what to do with the "extra" time? That's why it's so important to look in your rear view mirror. This perspective will show you where you want to end up. And once you establish this vision for your life, you'll know how to invest your time.

As I've said before, life is not a dress rehearsal. You only get one chance to live it. Make the path you take a meaningful one. And measure your success by your own yardstick, not one borrowed from someone else or society.

I wish for you the very best lifestyle possible, one full of adventure, interesting people, and varied activities. Have a wonderful trip through life with the people who matter to you.

ACTION NOTES

ACTION NOTES (continued)

ACTION NOTES (continued)

ACTION NOTES (continued)

TIME STATS

Working Longer

In 1973, the average work week, including commuting, was 41 hours. By 1989, the number had jumped to 47 hours.

And matters are not improving.

In a Louis Harris Survey (1993), the number of hours had climbed to 50.2 hours. In short, we're working more — and probably enjoying it less.

Junk Mail
The average American spends
7 years
reading junk mail.

Wasted Time
The average person wastes
45%
of their day.

Interruptions
The average office support person is interrupted
every 1 to 2 minutes.

Costly Memos

Memos are generally rewritten 4.2 times. As a result, the approximate cost to a company for each memo is $81.90.

(Personnel Journal)

Watching TV

Today's child will have spent approximately
7 years
watching television by the age of 70.

(American Academy of Pediatrics)

Busy-ness

Americans spend an average of 8 years attending business meetings and 2 years playing phone tag.

(Fortino Associates)

QUOTABLES

The Paradox of Time: We never seem to have enough time, yet we have all the time there is!

"Managing time means managing yourself in order to accomplish your goals within the time available."

Merrill Douglas

"The more you do of what you're doing, the more you'll get of what you've got."

Larry Baker

The Ten Things That Time Is

Economic Resource
Highly Perishable
Expensive
Inflexible
Measurable
Ongoing
Irreversible
Uninsurable
Irreplaceable
Democratic

ABOUT THE AUTHOR

Kay Johnson is President of Johnson West Associates, Inc., a problem-solving company for businesses and other organizations. She specializes in strategic planning, training, team building, and management evaluation and is a frequent speaker at conventions and conferences.

Kay is certified in negotiations from Harvard University and has a masters in education. Clients include IBM, Nabisco, USAir, Sara Lee, Hanes and 400 other companies across the country.

For more information about Johnson West Associates, please call 910-725-9465. Kay would appreciate hearing your comments about the book and the results you have with this method.

COMMENTS

Executives and community leaders endorse Kay Johnson's time management techniques.

"This was a dynamic and exciting approach to living. I am sure the things I learned will assist me as our company goes through change on a global scale."

Director, IBM

"We are stressed in our division because of downsizing and changes in the market. Your time management systems have opened a new way of living stress free in a very stressed world."

IS Team Leader, USAir

"I needed to learn not to get so over committed. Between patient care, resident education and research, there is difficulty allowing for family, soccer games and scouts. This has shown avenues for getting my life under control."

Anesthesiologist, Univ. of Texas Medical Center

"All successful executives should live by your time management systems. What an incredible impact — my whole life changed!"

CEO, Fast food chain

"We are much better equipped to schedule activities, prioritize them, and stick to our plans. The Time Management training we underwent was definitely successful!"

VP Administration, Bellomy Research

"The Time Management workshop was very effective. I clearly see a new attitude and cleaner desks in our offices."

Finance Director, Sara Lee Personal Products

"Kay's presentation was very enthusiastic and provided valuable materials and information which our people will find useful in planning and organizing. We would consider this seminar to be of value to any company."

Director of Corporate Services, Amarr Garage Doors

"I am currently working in a large organization where the ability to use time is extremely important. Your seminar helped me recognize and better understand how to work effectively with friends and co-workers."

Manager, Arthur Anderson

"I sincerely appreciate your Time Management seminar, and I feel confident that my employer and I will both reap benefits from your efforts for many years to come."

Manager, Dare County Airport

"You have given me a workable plan to make my life easier."

Administrator, First Southern Savings Bank

SERVICES OFFERED BY JOHNSON WEST ASSOCIATES

Training ☐
Custom-designed offerings in skill-building and various aspects of human behavior. We have designed 170 different courses for corporate clients of all sizes.

Needs Assessment ☐
One-on-one confidential interviews with employees to determine what's working and what's not within a department or company. A comprehensive written report including specific recommendations for improvement provides a valuable "snapshot" of performance, strengths and weaknesses.

Coaching Clinics ☐
One-on-one sessions for corporate executives, physicians, attorneys and other leaders in specific areas of interest such as career promotion, total quality management, advanced management techniques, and delegation.

Retreats ☐
Off-site seminars or planning sessions addressing specialized areas of concern in a fun, relaxed environment. Participants take an inside look at organizational missions, values, issues and problems, while focusing on practical, on-the-job improvements.

Strategic Planning ☐

An opportunity to look ahead through multifaceted planning sessions incorporating industry-specific information and research. Using any one of five Johnson West models for strategic planning, we look at vision, paradigms, purpose, values, strategies, and implementation to prepare for a global economy.

Facilitation/Focus Groups ☐

An impartial and unbiased approach to sensitive issues as we coordinate or direct meetings and discussions.

Mediation ☐

Services that bring two or more opposing viewpoints to the same table to work toward a solution. Bringing issues to positive closure, working on a planned outcome, and giving every side a hearing helps bring positive results.

For more information about the services
listed above, please tear out this page,
check the appropriate box or boxes and send
with your name, address and phone number to:

Johnson West Associates
245-B North Hawthorne Road
Winston-Salem, NC 27104-4302